His Word Is Among Us

Personal Encounters with God in Scripture

Louise Perrotta, Editor

the WORD among us®

The Word Among Us
9639 Doctor Perry Road
Ijamsville, Maryland 21754
www.wordamongus.org

Cover and book design: David Crosson
CNS photo by James Baca

Made and printed in the United States of America

Library of Congress Cataloging-in-Publication Data

His Word is among us : personal encounters with God in Scripture /
Louise Perrotta, editor.
    p. cm.
Includes bibliographical references and index.
  ISBN 1-59325-026-6 (alk. paper)
  1. Spiritual life—Catholic Church. 2. Bible—Devotional use. I.
Perrotta, Louise.
BX2350.3 .H57 2003
242'.5—dc22
                                                      2003022637

Table of Contents

Foreword

The people who tell their stories in *His Word Is Among Us* have discovered how the Bible differs from all other books. As they read its words, they met the Author who lives among its pages. That cannot happen with any other book.

In every other book the author must stay hidden behind the paper and ink. We cannot get to know him beyond what he reveals about himself in the text, which often is next to nothing. We cannot meet him unless we go to one of his lectures or book signings. We cannot ask him a question, dispute a point with him, or ask his help with a problem. As far as we can tell, he may as well be dead, even if he is very much alive.

But that's not the case with the Bible. When we open it, we are entering a place where the Author himself dwells. God welcomes us into his presence and, if we like, we can converse with him in prayer. He reveals himself to us so that we can get to know him. We can ask him what a passage means for us, and he gives us understanding about how to apply it to our lives. As the writers of this book tell in their stories, he does much more for us through Scripture.

The men, women, and children of *His Word Is Among Us* share heartwarming accounts of the way the Lord used the Bible to save them in their great needs. They tell how his Word resolved their serious problems, delivered them from addictions, opened them to the grace of healing, brought them to repentance, restored their relationships, and so on. I predict that their testimonies will have a profound effect on the way you approach the Bible. You will read it more personally, anticipating that the Author may have something to say to you. Or that he may be offering to do something for you. And as a result, you will come to know him more clearly, love him more dearly, and follow him more nearly, day by day.

Bert Ghezzi
Author, *Sacred Passages: Bringing the Sacraments to Life*

Introduction

Anyone who thirsts for God eagerly studies and meditates on the inspired word, knowing that there he is certain to find the One for whom he thirsts," wrote the medieval monk and Doctor of the Church, St. Bernard of Clairvaux. Eight centuries later, the bishops of the Second Vatican Council drew attention to this same truth: "In the sacred books the Father who is in heaven meets his children with great love and speaks with them" (*Dei Verbum*, 21).

The people who contributed the stories in this book know from experience that statements like these, which can be found throughout the history of the Church, point to the living, life-changing presence of God in the word of God. Their witnesses invite us to make this joyful discovery for ourselves.

The stories come from readers of *The Word Among Us,* a monthly magazine that features daily meditations on Scripture texts drawn from the Catholic liturgical readings for the day. Some of these contributors have been meeting the Lord in his word for a long time; others are just beginning the journey. Together, they represent quite a variety of approaches and experiences.

Here you'll find stories about Scripture's sustaining presence in joys and in sorrows, in ordinary and in extraordinary moments of life. Some describe an isolated incident or the impact of a single verse; others recount how a theme developed over time, sometimes by way of many Scripture passages.

You'll notice as you read that God has many ways of reaching us through his word. Maybe we're struck by a remark in a homily or a verse that "jumps off the page" when we open the Bible. Maybe the Holy Spirit brings a Scripture passage to mind as we're puzzling over a decision or struggling to understand something. God may act powerfully in us through a particular Scripture, or perhaps he leads us to a passage that sheds light on something we've already experienced.

In more ways than we can imagine, the Author of Scripture lovingly invites us to come and drink more deeply of his life-giving word. How can we do that? The stories in *The Word Is Among Us* offer a wealth of ideas. Here are some suggestions to consider, along with questions to stimulate your thinking:

Make yourself available. God can break into the most unsuspecting, unprepared hearts. At the same time, he awaits some sign of interest, especially from people who already have been awakened to him. Many of the scriptural encounters in this book come from men and women who made a decision to buy a Bible, pray and read Scripture regularly, or attend a retreat or conference. Ask yourself: *What next step can I take to express a "Here I am!" attitude of openness and desire?*

Try something new. Everyone goes through dry times when Scripture seems like a dead letter. The stories in this book suggest various revitalizing possibilities: take a Scripture class, keep a journal, join a Bible study group, memorize a weekly verse, seek out good publications, listen to music tapes or CDs featuring songs based on Scripture. Ask yourself: *What one new approach to Scripture could I implement?*

Don't go it alone. Meeting Jesus in his word means developing an intimate, personal relationship with him. This doesn't happen in isolation, however. We are members of the Church, the Body of Christ, and we need the Church's help as we seek to understand and apply Scripture for ourselves. The Holy Spirit will guide us in this, if we ask him. Ask yourself: *What could I do to open myself more fully to the action of the Holy Spirit? To the guidance of the Church?*

Be patient and persist. You'll notice that many stories in this book are sprinkled with phrases like "over time" and "after a while." They highlight two realities of Christian living: the often lengthy stretches when Scripture seems unfulfilled, and God's absolute faithfulness. Take heart! "Those who wait for the LORD shall renew their strength, they shall mount up with wings like eagles" (Isaiah 40:31). Ask yourself: *Am I in a waiting period right now? In what areas do I especially need to reassert my faith in God's promises?*

Welcome God's word into your daily life. The Word who came into our world through the Incarnation seeks entrance into every corner of our lives. By appropriating and applying Scripture in everyday situations and contacts, we cooperate with this plan. Our encounters with God's word should impact how we live and relate. Ask yourself: *Does my contact with Scripture affect the way I live? Do I follow listening with doing, as the Spirit leads?*

Pass the word along. "We cannot keep from speaking about what we have seen and heard," Peter and John told the religious authorities who were trying to muzzle their witnessing about Jesus (Acts 4:20). In a similar way, sharing our own encounters with the living Word can glorify God, build up the Body of Christ, and stir up a spirit of thanksgiving. It can also be a nonthreatening way to evangelize. Ask yourself: *How have I met God in Scripture? Where could I find opportunities to share about it with family, friends, or colleagues?*

Pray as you read. As the bishops at Vatican II wrote, "prayer should accompany the reading of sacred Scripture, so that God and man may talk together" (*Dei Verbum*, 25). Our reading should also inspire our praying. To meditate on Scripture is to consider what God has done, and this reflection overflows naturally into prayer. The Bible provides us with truths to ponder, with psalms, hymns, and other prayers to pray. It also helps us to enter more deeply into the greatest prayer of all, the celebration of the Eucharist.

In the Eucharist we enter into the central event of Scripture—Jesus' death and resurrection—and we experience the divine life into which Scripture guides us. The Eucharist brings us into communion with Jesus, the Word of God, and gives us the most profound opportunity to express our gratitude for his love. Ask yourself: *What can I do to approach Scripture more prayerfully? To grow in understanding and gratitude for the Eucharist as the table of God's Word?*

How to Use This Book. We've grouped the stories into twelve chapters, loosely arranged around twelve themes. Each chapter has a short introduction that includes points for reflection, as well as suggestions and Scripture verses to help you in your prayer time. Look through the table of contents, dip in here and there, or read chapter by chapter, as you feel inclined and the Spirit leads. If you feel drawn to prayer as you read, be sure to put the book down and pray!

Beginning on page 257, you'll find an index of the biblical passages mentioned in the book. We've listed them according to various themes so that you can draw on them more easily, according to your needs.

At the back of the book, you'll also find biographical notes about the people who contributed these stories. We are very grateful for their willingness to share about their encounters with God in Scripture. Their stories have built up our own faith and hope.

May they also lead you to a deeper encounter with the living Word who awaits you in the written word of God.

Louise Perrotta
Editor

1

Getting Free

Always and everywhere, we all need a Savior. But isn't it true that we know our need most keenly when we're experiencing our helplessness? These are the times when we're most likely to imitate the blind, the lepers, and all the other people who cried out to Jesus, "Lord, have mercy on me!" There were, of course, other gospel characters who should have cried out to Jesus but didn't. They couldn't (or wouldn't) admit their neediness.

The men and women who contributed the stories in this chapter had reason to cry out for deliverance from some unhealthy attitude, pattern, or addiction. Interestingly, however, several didn't know they had a problem until the Lord brought it to their attention!

What about you? Is this a season of crying out to God for needs that you are unable to meet on your own? Or could you use a stronger dose of self-knowledge? Whatever the case, let this chapter inspire you to open yourself more fully to your loving God.

Think About It!

"The spiritual battle requires self-knowledge," St. Ignatius Loyola wrote in his *Spiritual Exercises*. After all, we have an enemy who cunningly adapts his tactics to fit our basic orientation and weaknesses.

Let's keep in mind that self-knowledge and salvation come from the same source. Drawing close to the Lord will reveal us to ourselves:

> Let me know you, O you who know me; then I shall know, even as I am known. (Prayer of St. Augustine)

Pray It!

Jesus wants to deepen your experience and understanding of true freedom. Let his words of truth sink into you and have their full effect:

> Then Jesus said to the Jews who had believed in him, "If you continue in my word, you are truly my disciples; and you will know the truth, and the truth will make you free.... Very truly, I tell you, everyone who commits sin is a slave to sin.... If the Son makes you free, you will be free indeed." (John 8:31-32, 34, 36)

Called to Hope
By Terry P.*

With the eyes of your heart enlightened, you may know what is the hope to which he has called you. (Ephesians 1:18)

St. Paul's words struck my heart with a blow that brought tears to my eyes. I tore the page from the missalette and folded it into the palm of my hand, as if gripping it would assure my hanging on to the hope that Paul was talking about.

Three weeks without a drink. I was hanging on by my fingernails. I was at Sunday Mass on St. Croix in the Virgin Islands, on a long-planned vacation with friends. I had come armed with literature from the Alcoholics Anonymous program I had joined, but I despaired of ever getting what the A.A. people had—a sure faith in their "Higher Power" that they could stay sober, one day at a time.

Missalette in hand, I followed the first and second readings of the day. Then, as we stood for the Gospel, I heard the mind-blowing acclamation from Ephesians.

I was not struck sober. I continued to suffer because I wanted a drink so badly. But I did not drink. I wore out the torn missalette page on which was printed the promise of a hope of which I was not capable, willing my unwilling self to answer God's call.

Between swimming and sunning on the beach, I read my A.A. books and went to an A.A. meeting at Serenity House, across the road from "Kid Tough's Bar and Poolroom." I could hear the click of the pool balls and thought I could hear the drinks being poured as the A.A. speaker told us of the hope for a sober day that meetings gave him.

A million times that week, especially when ordering bottled water at cocktail time, I silently repeated the A.A. slogan: "The first drink gets you drunk." As badly as I wanted to drink, I did not want to be a drunk. And so, with all my heart, I prayed that the eyes of my heart would be enlightened so that I would know the hope to which God was calling me.

Back home to family, work, church, and A.A. meetings, I called to God more and more. Often I pounded on my desk at work as I prayed for hope that God's power would keep me from a drink for the next hour. Then, when the next hour came, I would pray, "Thank you for the last hour. Now you must give me your power in which I hope once again."

I got what I prayed for—the power not to drink, the power to be faithful to what I was learning in A.A. about changing the way I lived.

The gospel acclamation given to me in St. Croix became my prayer in the toughest, darkest moments: "Lord, please open me to the hope which is mine as your daughter." After three months, I realized one day that I had not thought of a drink for an entire morning, and I thanked God for the respite from the craving.

The hope to which God called me was moving from my head to my heart. It opened me more to God's power. It energized me to put one foot in front of another, to count my blessings and thank the Lord for keeping me sober each day.

I do not believe that the Lord made me a drunk. I do believe that God used my disease of alcoholism to get my attention, to remind me of what I was missing in my life and my faith, and to warn me of what I might lose if I kept drinking.

In one moment in that shuttered church in St. Croix, the Spirit grabbed my heart and opened my eyes that I might know that I had the right to hope in God's power to help me not to drink and to change. I know now that I can live as God means me to live—happy, joyous, and free. One day at a time, I thank God.

A pseudonym has been used at the author's request.

My Miracle of Healing

By Sr. Virgene Marx, O.S.B.

Ogden, Utah

Do you want to be healed? (John 5:6)

Six years ago, I began serving as a hospice chaplain. I was happy to be able to listen and pray with people as they faced the last months and days of their lives. Then one wintry November morning, as I hurried out of weekday Mass to attend a hospice meeting, I slipped on the church steps and broke my femur. Surgery and hospitalization followed. Within a few weeks, I had recovered enough to leave the hospital and continue my physical therapy exercises at the convent.

My leg continued to heal well as the weeks passed, but other difficulties surfaced. I became very fearful and depressed about real and imagined physical problems. Tests were done at the hospital, and all proved normal. However, my depression deepened to the point where I lost my desire to live. What was the use? There was no joy in anything—not music, reading, prayer, or anything else. Current events did not interest me anymore. I could not even envision my former joy of helping others. Finally, my religious superior and the doctor decided that it was time for me to see a psychiatrist. Because I was so miserable, I agreed.

The psychiatrist was very kind, listened attentively, and gave me sleeping pills. The sleeping pills helped me to sleep better, but when I woke up, the same depressed thoughts and feelings were there. There seemed to be no hope or joy or reason to live.

One day I was alone in my room, in bed and feeling depressed and sad. The sisters had gone to church, and I felt discouraged that I had not even been able to go with them. *How long can I handle this terrible feeling of depression?* I wondered. I looked around at my familiar surroundings—the ceiling, the window, my desk, and my wonderful maroon recliner. All seemed lifeless and cold. Then my eyes caught sight of the several bottles of pills on my dresser. What if I took all those pills at once? The more I looked at them, the more enticing became the thought of ending it all.

But then another thought crossed my mind. What impact would my suicide have on others? I considered the sorrow and grief of my family, the devastating pain I would cause the community of sisters with whom I live.

Standing on the narrow line between life and death, I wavered. If I crossed that line, I believed I would go to hell. I would also be going against everything I believed about life as a gift from God. In that critical moment, something pulled me back … the grace of God, no doubt.

The following weeks and months continued as before. I prayed as best I could and read Scripture, though there was no joy in it. God was silent and seemed far away. I believed he was with me, but I never felt his nearness.

One evening as I sat in my recliner, I picked up my Scripture and began to read a section from the New Testament. I was alone, but suddenly I heard a voice say to someone who seemed to be beside my chair, "Do you want to be healed?" I heard the voice answer clearly, "Yes." Then I saw a figure in front of me wearing a long, pure white gown full of folds from top to bottom. I could see no face, just this moderately tall someone. Then the figure asked me, "Do you want to be healed?" Quickly and loudly, I answered "YES!" Then the figure was gone.

I felt no different but was bewildered and did not know what to do. After a little while, I just went to bed.

I slept well and felt good the next morning. That was not too unusual. There had been other mornings when I had felt good for a short time, only to have all the terrible feelings and thoughts come back later. *It won't be long now,* I thought, waiting for them to hit again.

One hour went by, then two, and I was still upbeat. I felt good and wanted to do things and even help where I could. As the day went on, I checked myself every hour. *Isn't this great,* I thought with amazement. *I feel so good!* After a few days had passed, I knew I was myself again. God had come and healed me! I was eager to work in the convent and cook or do whatever needed to be done.

I felt I needed to tell the other sisters but hesitated because of what they might say or think. After several days, as I sat at table with some of them, I explained that I was healed. They looked at me, wondering what was going on with me now. Finally, Sister Mary, our prioress, asked Sister Luke—who spent the most time with me—if I was really different. "Oh yes," Sister Luke replied in her dry, humorous way. "She is her old 'crummy' self!"

This took place almost five years ago now, and I continue to feel well and find life beautiful in every respect. A current comment from people who know me is, "You look so good!" My health has improved, and I am looking forward to celebrating my eighty-second birthday. My gratitude to God knows no bounds!

Praying for the Enemy
By Gabriel Harkay
Lakeside, California

Forgive us our debts, as we also have forgiven our debtors.
(Matthew 6:12)

The retreat master's words on the importance of forgiveness sounded familiar. In fact they seemed so familiar that I almost put them on the back burner. He was elaborating on the words of Jesus in Matthew 6:12: "Forgive us our trespasses, as we forgive those who trespass against us."

Oh yes, I knew that forgiveness is so important that Jesus made it an indispensable condition of our own salvation. I knew that if we pray the *Our Father* without forgiving others, we're asking God not to forgive us either. And I knew that anyone whose sins are not forgiven is in big trouble! *But I don't hate anybody,* I thought. *This shouldn't concern me too much....*

As we sat there, in a conference hall at Mission San Luis Rey in California, the retreat master went on, elaborating on the possibility of hidden resentment that can choke the free flow of grace. As an exercise, he told us to close our eyes and think of someone who had hurt us and then to pray for that person. I followed his instructions, and wartime pictures suddenly began appearing in my mind. I saw fire and destruction and the enemy—Russian soldiers. I was feeling terror. I was also feeling my rifle in my hands. I tried to pray for the soldiers, but it was impossible. All I wanted was to kill them.

This painful moment went back to some traumatic experiences I had during World War II, as cities were bombed mercilessly and the Hungarian army was desperately fighting the invading Soviet forces. I was a prisoner of war at age sixteen. Then after returning to Hungary, I lived for three years under Communist terror. Finally I had to flee to the West. I wasn't aware of how much anxiety and hatred had been buried deep inside me, but I had nightmares and often woke up at night soaked in cold sweat. Whenever the subject of the Soviets came up in conversation, I always got very angry. And somehow, I had the feeling that it was patriotic to hate the "enemy."

The retreat master brought the session to a close, and we broke for lunch. In the dining hall, some other retreatants and I discussed the talk and shared what had happened during the forgiveness exercise. I said what a painful episode it had been for me and admitted that I simply couldn't pray for the Russians.

"Those old hurts can be healed," said a young lady who was sitting across the table. "For Jesus, those past experiences are like all in the present. Why not ask Jesus to come into your past and touch those hurts with his healing hands?"

"Okay," I said. I stopped eating my bowl of salad and put down my fork. Very simply, I invited Jesus to come into my painful memories.

Suddenly I started to sob uncontrollably. My tears flowed, and I kept sobbing—for a long time, it seemed. I felt a great pressure being relieved. I can only compare it to that moment when you're skin diving with a snorkel and running out of air and shooting for the surface ... and finally you make it! The pressure is gone, and you can take a big, deep breath.

I wiped my face and looked up. The young lady was standing behind me and praying over me. Bewildered, I stood up and mumbled some words of thanks, then walked out into the beautiful garden in the back to reflect on what had happened. I was still recalling those wartime images and seeing the violence and destruction—but now they were not chewing me up inside. They were not hurting anymore.

A long time before, a psychologist had told me that my wartime experiences were at the root of my short temper and my stomach ulcer. Talking about the war with him had not made the stress go away. But the healing touch of Jesus took away a hatred I had never recognized and made me able to forgive "the enemy." My nightmares and cold sweats have disappeared. I'm so grateful for this healing. A new horizon has opened for me, and I can grow.

I have come to realize that there will always be some anxiety in my life but that I can cope with the peace Jesus gives. To be honest, I still don't like or trust the "Russian Bear"—but I can sure pray for the people of Russia! I can also forgive current hurts much more easily, and I have really started to practice St. Paul's instruction not to let the sun go down on my anger (Ephesians 4:26).

I no longer simply rattle off that forgiveness clause in the *Our Father*. Now I take time in my prayers to search out any trace of anger in me and to think of people who may have hurt me. *That guy who cut me off on the road and almost scraped my fender— I had to bite my tongue to keep from blurting out some colorful language at him. Can I forgive him? Can I bless him? Can I pray that God envelop him with his love? Yes, I have to.*

There is still a long way to go, but I keep trying. There is no better way.

The Peach Tree
By Lillian Valencia
Bloomfield, New Mexico

He will command his angels ... to guard you in all your ways. (Psalm 91:11)

I would like to share my story in hopes that it will help someone who is afraid of heights.

My son was on a wrestling team, and I liked to watch him compete. My fear of heights was so bad, however, that I dreaded traveling to his out-of-town meets. The worst was when this meant having to go over Wolf Creek Pass in Colorado's San Juan Mountains.

The pass is high—10,850 feet at the very top—but the highway is very good. Whenever we drove this way, though, all I could see was fear. I would ride covered up in the back seat. I could not stand for anyone to touch me or talk to me until we were over the pass. For a week before and after the trip, I would have nightmares of falling off the mountain.

I tried everything. Drinking—couldn't get drunk. Sleeping pills—couldn't sleep. Praying—the words were not there. Singing—couldn't remember the words. I used to go along anyway but was too terrified to enjoy the natural beauty that God had given us. My fear kept me from seeing many scenic views of mountains and rivers.

One day I received the news that my cousin Rosie had been called home by God. I had grown up with her and other cousins on a farm; we all had a very close relationship with each other and always kept in touch. I wanted desperately to go to her Mass and funeral in Denver, but—yes, you guessed it—it would mean going over Wolf Creek Pass.

"Are you going with us?" my older sister asked me. She and two other sisters were planning to attend.

"Well, I'd like to, but…" My sisters didn't reproach me. They all knew about my fear.

I have a peach tree in my backyard. In the summer, that is where I have my prayer time with Jesus. I take a walk, then pick up a cup of coffee and ask Jesus to join me for a cup. This one morning, as I was walking, I talked to Jesus about this trip. "I want to go, Jesus, but I am so afraid." He didn't respond until we got back to the peach tree. I opened my Bible, and there before me was Psalm 91. I call it my "hug from the Lord."

As I read it, the message jumped out at me, especially verse 11: "He will command his angels to guard you in all your ways." *Command!* The impact was so strong I almost reeled! In one sudden moment, I felt such a freedom! I couldn't believe what was happening as I called my sister and said, "I am going to Denver with you guys."

"Are you sure?" she asked.

"Yes," I assured her, and told her about my experience with Psalm 91.

I went over Wolf Creek Pass and felt no fear. I even looked over the side. "Oh my, it isn't that high," I exclaimed. "Oh, how beautiful!"

Three years ago, I got on a plane—my first time—to visit my son in Oklahoma for Christmas. What a wonderful ride!

Free at last! Free at last! Thank you, God. He is my refuge, my fortress, my God in whom I trust.

Soaps and Scripture
By Janice Carleton
Portland, Oregon

Whatever is true, whatever is honorable, whatever is just, whatever is pure, whatever is pleasing, whatever is commendable, if there is any excellence and if there is anything worthy of praise, think about these things. (Philippians 4:8)

I grew up watching a soap opera with my mom. I felt like I knew everyone on the show, and I really enjoyed it. I continued our tradition while I was in college and also after I was married and had my first two children. After watching faithfully for eighteen years, the characters had become like a second family to me. I cried with them and laughed with them (well, mostly cried), and I looked forward to "my" show every day. Then one evening I went to a class at our church that changed my viewing habits.

The class was called "Hearing God through Scripture," and it was being taught by a good friend of mine. Steve explained to us that whenever we read Scripture we should invite the Holy Spirit to teach us, and we should open our hearts to allow the Lord to speak to us. After the instruction, he said, "Now let's try it!" He read a passage from Philippians 4. Verse 8 really got my attention: "Finally, beloved, whatever is true, whatever is honorable, whatever is just, whatever is pure, whatever is pleasing, whatever is commendable, if there is any excellence and if there is anything worthy of praise, think about these things."

Steve then asked us to wait in silence and let the Lord speak to us. As soon as he said those words, I heard the Lord ask me, "So, what about your soap opera? Is there anything honest, decent, virtuous, or admirable in it?"

I replied, "No, Lord."

Then he asked me, "So what are you going to do about it?"

I quickly promised to quit watching it. After the period of reflection I shared what I had heard. I remember others being surprised about the message—"What's so bad about soap operas?"—but I was determined. I even asked them to help me keep my promise.

I went home totally excited that the Lord had spoken to me. I didn't know that the God of the universe could speak to me about my life right now! I immediately shared the news with my husband and my little boys. I told the boys that if they happened to see Mommy watching "her" show, they were supposed to remind me that God told me not to watch it any more.

For the first week I didn't watch the show, but then I thought I should sneak just a peek to make sure everybody was okay—and to see if "Julie" and "Doug" were still together! I turned on the set. Almost immediately, John, who was two at the time, walked into the room and stood in front of the TV. He put his hands on his hips and said, "God told you not to watch this anymore!" I hugged and thanked him and turned off the set. That was the last time I turned it on or was even tempted.

This all happened shortly after we had moved to California from Oregon, and I realized that watching the show every day had interfered with making new friends. The Lord not only helped me give up my addiction, but he helped me to get on with my life by getting involved in my new church community. I also learned the importance of accountability. Since I had told other people what I was trying to do, God was able to help me through them.

God is so good! That was the first time the Lord spoke to me through Scripture, but it definitely hasn't been the last. Thank you, Lord!

Jesus Helped Me Quit!
By A Great-grandmother*
Combermere, Ontario, Canada

I waited patiently for the LORD;
he inclined to me and heard my cry. (Psalm 40:1)

When I was in eighth grade, I grew so quickly that I towered over most of my classmates. I also developed an insatiable appetite that caused an ongoing battle with my weight. By the time I graduated from high school, it had become readily apparent to me that smoking cigarettes could alleviate the problem.

Quite happily, I relied on cigarettes to replace second helpings and between-meal snacks. Besides, I saw smoking as a heaven-sent crutch for my teenage shyness, social awkwardness, and fragile self-esteem. In no time, I was so gladly hooked that I couldn't even imagine being happy in heaven without smoking! Little did I realize that this "perfect" cure would turn into thirty years of a seemingly hopeless struggle to be set free. Eventually I married a pipe smoker who also enjoyed the odd cigarette. But four children later, there came an agonizing problem: the children *hated* smoking. Because of this, I got into the habit of sneaking away to a hiding place to enjoy a cigarette. But there was no enjoyment in it. I was terrified of discovery and despised myself for my cowardice and deceit. Any satisfaction or pleasure I felt was almost completely nullified by fear and self-loathing. Thus motivated, for thirty years I tried everything to break the habit. Novenas, healing prayers, prayers for deliverance—nothing seemed to help for very long.

Finally, on August 15, 1992, the feast of Mary's Assumption, I complained seriously and earnestly to God. "Lord, I can quit anytime, but I always start up again because I just can't lose the *desire* to smoke. Please, please, you have to help me!"

The very next day, Sunday, August 16, the responsorial psalm nearly jumped off the page: "I need you, Lord. Come quickly to my aid. I waited, I waited for the Lord, and he stooped toward me; he heard my cry" (Psalm 40:1). Over the next week, during each day's Mass, the Lord spoke to me these words of hope:

Monday, August 17: Mass opened with "Lord, your mercy is my hope. My heart rejoices in your saving power."

Tuesday, August 18: The opening prayer was, "The Lord has been my strength; he has led me into freedom. He saved me because he loves me." It continued, "Let them not say: our own power wins the victory."

Wednesday, August 19: The entrance antiphon was from Psalm 24: "Look at me and be merciful, for I am wretched and alone. See my hardship and my poverty," and the opening prayer continued: "Father, your love never fails. Hear our call." The Communion antiphon promised: "Whatever you ask for in prayer, believe that you have received it, and it will be yours."

Thursday, August 20: The reading from Ezekiel 36 assured us: "I shall pour clean water over you. You will be cleansed of your defilement and all your idols."

Friday, August 21: Psalm 107 proclaimed: "Then they cried to the Lord in their need and he rescued them from their distress."

Saturday, August 22, the Queenship of Mary: Isaiah 9 declared: "For the yoke that was weighing on him, the bar across his shoulder, the rod of his oppressor, these you break as on the day of Midian." In Luke's Gospel we heard the angel Gabriel telling Mary: "For nothing is impossible with God."

Sunday, August 23: The opening verse was from Psalm 85: "Listen, Lord, and answer me. Save your servant who trusts in you. I call to you all day long. Have mercy on me, Lord."

By the end of this week of intensive immersion in Scripture's words of hope, I found I didn't care if I *never* saw a cigarette again! I quit smoking without any difficulty.

The following February, my dear husband died. Formerly, something like this would certainly have driven me to reach for a calming cigarette. I never even *thought* of it. Through the power of God's word, I had received real, total deliverance.

Dear Jesus, thank you with all my heart. I can never praise you enough!

A pseudonym has been used at the author's request.

The Gift of Peace

By Norma J. Matasich

Hampstead, North Carolina

Nothing will ever be able to separate us from the love of God demonstrated by our Lord Jesus Christ.
(Romans 8:39, The Way: Catholic edition)

When I was about eleven or twelve, I slowly became aware of the broader world and the dangers and evils that are out there—especially nuclear weapons. During those times there was much talk of the arms race and of our superpower counterpart, the U.S.S.R. The papers often reported on it, and it was a topic of conversation in my family. I remember a commercial that featured a little blonde girl sitting on a stool, and then a picture of a mushroom cloud. It was an era of "No Nukes!" protests and demonstrations against "Mutually Assured Destruction." Like many other people my age, I had an unsettling sense that at the push of a button—poof, the world would end.

This gave me such a deep-seated fear that I never knew how to express it. I don't recall sharing these feelings with anyone. Among my friends there were occasional comments about nuclear war, but they were followed by a quick change of subject to avoid dampening our mood.

Each night when I said my prayers, however, I would ask Jesus to dismantle those bombs. This subject always entered into my prayer life and my meditations, especially when I was out in the mountains or in my backyard, watching birds flying or simply observing an anthill. I would be admiring God's creation and a thought would creep in: "O Lord, if such an evil thing as nuclear war were to happen, surely you would just call it quits on us human beings. That would be the end of it. You'd probably say, 'I've had it! I've given them all of this, and continually they turn away. I came down from heaven and died for their sins, yet still they commit crimes against each other and destroy the creation I gave them dominion over. And now this incredible evil of blowing up the very world I made—that's it!'"

This fear persisted throughout high school, and took hold of me even more when I was about twenty, married, and with a new baby. Now there was a new life to be concerned with, a little person with her whole life ahead of her. I would sit in my rocker, holding her and admiring her face, her tiny fingers, the way she moved her mouth, the warmth of her body. Though my thoughts naturally turned to prayer, I was increasingly fearful.

I usually read Scripture during my prayers, turning first to Proverbs and then to the gospels. One day, though, I decided to read Romans 8. Verses 37, 38, and 39 stopped me in my tracks: "But despite all this, overwhelming victory is ours through Christ who loved us enough to die for us. For I am convinced that nothing can ever separate us from his love. Death can't and life can't. The angels won't and all the powers of hell itself cannot keep God's love away—nothing will ever be able to separate us from the love of God demonstrated by our Lord Jesus Christ when he died for us."

Wow! "Not all the powers of hell!" To me, of course, the worst that hell could send us would be the utter destruction of creation through nuclear holocaust. And now I knew that even this would not cause God to turn away. From within the deepest part of me, I knew without a doubt that the Holy Spirit had spoken to me. It wasn't an audible voice or vision—just an overpowering sense of serenity, peace, and the knowledge that I had been heard and answered. My deep, nagging, unspoken fears went away, never to return.

Why did God wait eight years before giving me this gift? All I know is that God answers us on his terms and timetable, not ours. I continue to pray for peace—I always will—but the crippling fear is gone. Whatever happens on the world scene, I know the Lord has the final say and that he won't call it quits on us.

I have been married for nineteen years now. That little baby is eighteen and attending college, and I have three younger children. My life has its ups and downs, but the older I get, the stronger my faith grows and the more alive the Bible becomes to me. What awesome peace we have through Christ and his word! "The light shines in the darkness, and the darkness has not overcome it" (John 1:5).

2

"I Am with You"

In his book, *Beginning to Pray*, the Russian Orthodox arch-bishop and spiritual writer Anthony Bloom described himself as "an unbeliever and very aggressively anti-church" until, in his teens, he picked up the New Testament for the first time. He wasn't in the most receptive mood. A talk by a priest, which he had attended out of courtesy to a friend, had given him a glimpse of Christianity that disturbed him. Indignantly, looking for a fight, he began reading the Gospel of Mark.

He hadn't even gotten to chapter three, he says, when "I suddenly became aware that on the other side of my desk there was a presence. And the certainty was so strong that it was Christ standing there that it has never left me. This was the real turning point."

In this chapter, you'll find evidence that Jesus is with us always and that he will never abandon us once we've made our decision to follow him. Even when we feel lonely, desperate, fearful, confused, or longing to see him more clearly, Jesus is right there with us, as he said he'd always be.

Think About It!

Do you sometimes feel like God is a million miles away? St. Jane de Chantal knew that feeling too, because she experienced decades of spiritual dryness. Even in the midst of it, though, she was known for her joyful faith. The reason? She believed without a doubt that God is faithful to his promises. "We are in the world as poor blind men," she said. "We don't see our Lord, but faith teaches us that God is present in all things and that he dwells in our hearts in a particular way...." Something to remember the next time you begin to wonder where the Lord has gone!

Pray It!

In Matthew's Gospel, the first we hear about Jesus—in the angel's announcement of his birth—is that he will be "God with us." In the Gospel's very last verse, we have Jesus' own word for it. Where in your life do you most need this assurance right now? Let these verses inspire your prayer, as you bring your thanks and requests to God:

Look, the virgin shall conceive and bear a son, and they shall name him Emmanuel, which means, "God is with us." (Matthew 1:23)

And remember, I am with you always, to the end of the age. (Matthew 28:20)

Antidote for Loneliness
By Ken Watson*

O Lord, you have searched me and known me.
You know when I sit down and when I rise up;
you discern my thoughts from far away. (Psalm 139:1-2)

Loneliness is a disease of our age. In spite of—or because of—our efforts to do everything and to know everything and everyone, we can often feel empty. I am no different. I recently finished a two-year graduate program in journalism, in a town hundreds of miles from home. While there were always people within easy reach, it was hard not to feel isolated at times.

But I learned that I was not really alone. In fact, it seemed that God was even more interested in letting me know he was with me than I was in trying to find him! One experience in particular stands out.

I had the stomach flu. It wasn't so much the flu that bothered me, though, as the absence of friends. It seemed like everyone who had promised to call me hadn't called. There was nothing for me to do but lie there and think about life back home, where I had a whole network of people I could depend on. "What am I even here for?" I asked the Lord. "Is this really your will? Did you really want me to move out here and study this stuff? What's the point?" Just about the time I was sinking into total self-pity, someone knocked on the door of my apartment. In a year and a half, no one had knocked on my door unless I had buzzed them up from the front door of the building. I opened to find my next-door neighbor holding a package that had gotten mixed up in her mail. It was addressed to me. I looked at the return address and saw that it was from Dave, one of my best friends in the world.

A few months before, Dave had promised to make me an audiotape of some of his comic routines. This was it. Besides being a great friend, Dave has an unusual sense of humor. In person, he can often cause me to convulse with laughter without his even trying. I got back in bed, turned on the tape, and listened to Dave ramble. He had recorded the tape in his car and, as is his custom, was doing hilarious imitations of various celebrities. As the tape continued, the phone rang. I lumbered across the dark living room and picked up the receiver to find that the voice on the other end of the line was none other than Dave's. I told Dave to hold on while I turned off the tape in the other room, because I couldn't handle him in stereo! We were both amazed at the coincidence. We talked about the weather and about whatever came into our heads—I was so happy to talk to Dave that the subject didn't really matter.

When I hung up, I realized that the phone call had not been mere coincidence. As with other experiences I could think of, it was an instance of the Lord showing me that he knew absolutely everything I was going through. In this case, he used a close friend to surprise me with his kindness and closeness to me even when I felt most abandoned. But why was I surprised? One of my favorite Scripture passages, Psalm 139, tells us that God knows when we sit and when we stand, that he knows our going out and our lying down; he even knows the words we are going to say before they are on our lips. God knew us, the psalmist says, even before we were born.

That psalm, by "chance," was one Dave had quoted to me in a letter he had sent a few months earlier. His letter came on the same day a priest had told me to read one of the psalms. Which one? Psalm 139, of course.

Pseudonym used at the author's request.

Discovering "God with Us"
By Joanne Dugan
Crescent Springs, Kentucky

*They shall name him Emmanuel, which means
"God is with us." (Matthew 1:23)*

Ever since I can remember, God's word in Scripture has been an important part of my life. I was a second-grader at Sacred Heart School when the "Emmanuel" message in the Christmas pageant snuggled warmly in my heart. Later, in a freshman religion class at St. Xavier Academy, I read Matthew 28:20. "I am with you always, yes, to the end of time" (*Jerusalem Bible*) became God's personal promise to me.

As I've moved through the different stages of my life, the awareness of God's presence has grown. Emmanuel is no longer just a word. It is *the* Word. He is with me, if I only open my eyes to his daily gifts.

Emmanuel walked with me as I watched my mom minister to an aunt who was dying of cancer, as my younger sister left our home to discern if religious life was her vocation, as I grappled with a broken engagement, and as I mourned my father's death from a heart attack at age fifty-five. I saw his hand in my marriage to Jim. And when my mother—only fifty-one years old—died nine months after our wedding, Emmanuel was present in our decision to invite my twelve-year-old brother to live with us.

In the miracles of the births of our children and in the sadness of two miscarriages, he was there. How else could I explain the relative calm and patience I maintained as we raised five children, moving often as Jim's job changed? Emmanuel was my strength during all the storms when the kids were in their teens and we were "ruining their lives" with all our rules.

I smile as I recall another blessing. Jim and I hungered to attend a charismatic renewal conference in Ireland in June 1978, but the cost was beyond us—a staggering $1,400. Then we got our income tax refund. It was $1,440! My cup overflowed.

I remember an October morning when I really needed the assurance of Emmanuel's presence. The leaves were dressed in their finest, fiery burnt oranges, bright yellows, and rust. The world was a beautiful place, but I wasn't happy. A tiff earlier in the week had wrinkled the communication between Jim and me, and the canyon of silence was expanding. I felt unloved, unwanted, and unappreciated. I asked God to show me that somebody cared and went on to specify just how he should handle this request—by letting me hear from someone "far away." As the day wore on, I began to suspect that God's response might be for me to "wait."

After the six o'clock anchor had replayed the news of the day, the phone rang. It was Jackie, my dear friend and sister-in-law from Pennsylvania. She said she had been thinking of me for weeks but "seemed to get a nudge this morning to call Jo today." The next day, the postman delivered a letter from my Aunt Edna, and my brother phoned just to chat. Two days later, I looked inside the mailbox and found a "you are special" card from my sister. I was flooded with the knowledge of God's presence. "Thanks," I told him. "I got your message." Jim and I mended our fences.

God—Emmanuel—is always there, both when I know I need him and when I think I'm managing well on my own. I sometimes feel his presence in thoughts that reassure my heart: "I will give you my words, when your words seem to fail you. I will give you my love, when you feel you no longer have any love of your own to give. I will carry you in your sorrow. I will lift you up in your joys, rejoicing with you as a father lifts up his child with delight. I will comfort you and console you. I have chosen you. You are mine."

I've also found God present in the people he sends into my life, who make me feel at home wherever I am. I've found Emmanuel in his people in Pennsylvania, Missouri, Michigan, Ohio, and Indiana, where we've lived. Even in my brief visits on vacation, his face has poked through Linda in Nevada, Beth in California, Mary and Vicki in Florida. I find him personally at Mass and in the sick and elderly to whom I bring the Eucharist.

As I learn more and more about Emmanuel and open my eyes to his daily gifts, it just gets better and better. He is indeed with me, if I only stop, look, and listen for him. My widowed ninety-seven-year-old friend, Orienda, summed it up perfectly: "I may be alone, but I'm not lonely. God is with me."

Up Close and Personal
By Flora De La Torre
Globe, Arizona

See that it is I myself. Touch me and see. (Luke 24:39)

My mother was very devoted to her Catholic faith. She prayed constantly, using many aids to prayer. No matter where she was, she always had her statues, religious images, rosary, missal, and candles.

I learned a lot from my mother and am following her example. There are members of my family, however, who have gone in different directions. Some no longer attend Sunday Mass or receive the sacraments. Some have married outside the Catholic Church.

One of these relatives, a long-lost cousin, came to see me one day while I was visiting one of my daughters. He noticed that I was wearing a medal, one I have had for forty-two years. It is a clasp pin with the image of Our Blessed Mother, the Immaculate Conception. I was not aware that this cousin had become an evangelist in a church that is hostile to Catholicism, but I soon found out. He grew irate and started accusing Catholics of putting their faith in "graven images." He wanted to "take me to the river" and rebaptize me then and there! I stood my ground. His outburst did not weaken my faith, but it left me feeling emotionally drained.

That night as I was praying to Jesus, I felt the need to be reassured that he was as real as the statue before me. The next thing I remember is that I seemed to see Jesus standing by my bed, holding out his arms to me and saying, "Touch me, I am real!" How loving Jesus is! He answered my prayer and let me know that he is always with us in a very real way, no matter what! I have felt his presence, and it will sustain me until the day I die.

His Grace Is Sufficient
By Uche Mercy Okonkwo
Lagos, Nigeria

My grace is sufficient for you, for my strength is made perfect in weakness. (2 Corinthians 12:9)

It was a Monday in late January 1999. I had just returned home from a long day that ended with a management meeting of heads of academic programs in one of the departments in the university where I worked. Famished, I was hurrying into my apartment to get something to eat when my eyes fell on a piece of paper stuck in the keyhole. It was a note asking me to see a friend as soon as I arrived home.

I quickly ate and then dashed off to see this friend. After the normal exchange of pleasantries, there followed some moments of silence. I noticed that my friend looked very worried and uncomfortable. Finally, when I could no longer bear the awkward silence, I asked if anything was the matter. She said nothing for a moment, but her look made it obvious that the matter was indeed very grave. Suddenly I got the message. "Have I been retired?" I asked. Her affirmative answer sent shivers through me. Now I realized that I was among the many people on the academic staff whose services were terminated because of some restructuring policy of the university.

I left and drove straight to my church on the university campus for evening Mass. The first reading was being proclaimed as I arrived, and I knelt down to say a short prayer. I cannot recall exactly what I prayed, but I remember that my heart was heavy with grief. Then the Lord's voice came to me very clearly: "My grace is sufficient for you." I knew that this verse was from 2 Corinthians, where St. Paul pleaded with the Lord to remove a difficulty—a "thorn"—that was causing him distress. My immediate response was, "Lord, if you say so, then you are in this with me." I wiped away the tears that were running down my cheeks. As if to confirm the Lord's message, the choir sang two hymns whose choruses also comforted and calmed me: "Trust and obey, for there is no other way to be happy in Jesus," and "It is well, it is well with my soul."

When I returned home, I read 2 Corinthians 12:7-10 and prayed fervently that the Lord would strengthen me as he had St. Paul. I then went to bed but could not sleep. It was the darkest night of my life—even darker than the night after a fire destroyed my car on the highway eight years before. That had been painful too, but at least I had the consolation of a job and a roof over my head. This was a different kettle of fish. No job meant no home and no secure future! With a thousand questions going through my head, sleep was fitful.

In the morning, I went to the office to clear away the outstanding work on my desk. Friends and colleagues offered sympathy as I collected my letter of retirement and then headed for home. "Why am I being treated like this?" I wondered. After all, I had served the university conscientiously for twenty-three years. My Christian faith was being put to a severe test.

As I gradually came to terms with my situation, I was hit by yet another crisis. Shortly after my retirement, the university asked me to vacate the residence they had provided. Since I was already building a house on land that some relatives had given me in my home state, I decided to accelerate its construction. But in March 1999 when I went home to inspect the house, the relatives who had suggested that I build there told me I should discontinue the project. My protests fell on deaf ears. As painful as the loss of my job had been, this denial of shelter in my time of need was even more so.

Another night of troubled sleep was followed by days of wondering what was really happening to me. Where was God in all this? Still, I kept reading Scripture and found much consolation there. As bad as this crisis was, I experienced a surprising inner peace.

With one phone call, my housing crisis came to an end. My older sister invited me to live with her and her family, and I have been there since August 1999. Even though it was some time before I found a regular full-time job, the Lord was graciously faithful in supplying my needs. In May 2003, God provided me with a full-time permanent job in an upcoming and fast-growing university here in Lagos.

Looking back on this jobless period, I recognize that it had many downs, but also many ups. It was very fruitful for me spiritually. I drew closer to God. My Bible has remained my daily companion, my source of comfort and assurance of God's reality and faithfulness. Remembering that God comforted "small me" with the same words he used to comfort the "great St. Paul" makes me feel very, very special. I know that I can have hope even when the future seems bleak, because I know that the Lord will never leave or forsake me (Hebrews 13:5). His grace is truly "sufficient"!

Centered on the Eucharist
By Gunda L. Neary
Litchfield Park, Arizona

Those who eat my flesh and drink my blood have eternal life, and I will raise them up on the last day. (John 6:54)

I was born in Nuremberg, Germany. My father died in the Second World War, and soon after, my mother became a Jehovah's Witness. Although I had been baptized in the Lutheran Church and also had made my First Communion there, I was no longer encouraged to attend.

This pattern of nonattendance continued after I emigrated to the United States and married an American who had been baptized and confirmed in the Catholic Church. We were blessed with two daughters and had them baptized in the Catholic Church, but that was as far as we went. Sadly, for them and for us, we never thought of attending church.

In the ups and downs of the following years, I found myself searching for inner peace. At my mother's request, I studied the Bible with the Jehovah's Witnesses, but their beliefs could not satisfy my heart. They taught that only 144,000 people with a special heavenly hope could partake at the Lord's table, and only once

a year at Passover time. It didn't seem right to me that the rest of
the congregation should be denied. Hadn't Jesus called himself the
bread of life and invited everyone to his table? Hadn't he promised that all those "who eat my flesh and drink my blood have
eternal life, and I will raise them up on the last day" (John 6:54)?

When I was forty years old, an evangelical Christian came to
my door to talk to me about Jesus. After a few visits, she asked
if I would kneel down with her and receive the Lord into my heart
as my Savior. With childlike faith, I agreed. Gradually a great
change took place in me. The Holy Spirit came into my life and
guided me gently and lovingly on my spiritual journey. Through
my Christian friend, I joined a little Baptist church nearby. I gained
much knowledge about the Bible there, and I loved the people.
It disturbed me, however, that Communion services were held only
once or twice a month and that there was no emphasis on the
Lord's "real presence."

After two years I joined a charismatic, nondenominational
church and stayed there for more than twenty years. I learned
much in many areas, and again I loved the people. Still, my heart
was not fully satisfied. There, too, Communion was given only
once a month, in the form of little crackers and grape juice. I did
not want to change churches again, but because of my unrest
about the Eucharist, my search continued.

I started to read books on the lives of the great saints in the
Catholic Church and was struck by their love and devotion to the
Eucharist. Finally, after much prayer, I signed up for instruction
classes. On Easter Day 1997, I was received into the Catholic
Church and was able to receive the holy Eucharist, the Lord's own
Body and Blood.

I have finally found the greatest treasure there is. Now the Lord
himself is nourishing me and keeps me spiritually alive for eternity. My spiritual journey is ongoing, but my search for peace is

over. In the most holy Eucharist, I have found the most holy center of my life.

God Has a Human Face
By Marita Kiley*

Even the hairs of your head are all counted. So do not be afraid.
(Matthew 10:30-31)

He looked so small and helpless lying face up in that hospital bed. The crisp, laundered sheets covered his little body, and I could barely see his face peering over them. His big brown eyes, wide with fear, took in every detail of these unfamiliar surroundings—unknown medical staff moving about in all directions, machines beeping, intimidating technology everywhere he looked.

"Mommy," Jonathan whispered, "I'm feeling all better now. Look, I can hear you just fine. Try me."

It was his one last attempt to escape the inevitable. Months of planning and careful hearing evaluations had all led to this very moment.

"I'm glad you're feeling and hearing better today, Jonathan, but we have to take care of this now, before there is any severe damage to your inner ear," I responded.

The last glimmer of hope drained from my son's face. He covered his face with the sheet and began to cry—soft, muffled sobs that resounded like thunder in my heart. He was scheduled for a simple outpatient procedure that we hoped would alleviate the effects of many ear infections and major hearing loss. But to this frightened ten-year-old, it might as well have been major heart surgery. I leaned over and held him close for what seemed like an eternity.

"I'm scared, Mommy," he mumbled. "I'm really, really scared."

"I know, Jonathan, but it's going to be okay. It really is. You're not alone, sweetie. God is always with you, and he is with you right now. You have to believe it in your heart."

He wiped away the tears and sat up in bed. "Mom, will you tell me a story?" he asked.

"Jonathan," I replied, "I'll do better than that." I reached down into my purse and pulled out an old, worn pocket Bible that my mother had given me many years before. "Let's see what the Lord has to say to us today."

I randomly opened my little book, not knowing what I was going to read but praying that the Holy Spirit would guide me as he had so many times before. I opened up to Matthew 10: 29-31. "Listen to this, Jonathan. God is speaking to you:

Are not two sparrows sold for a penny? Yet not one of them will fall to the ground apart from your Father. And even the hairs of your head are all counted. So do not be afraid; you are of more value than many sparrows.

His eyes perked up as his face broke out in a crooked little grin. "That's funny, Mom. He counted every hair on my head?"

"Every single one. God knows you and loves you better than anyone ever could, and he'll never abandon you." We laughed and joked as we tried counting hairs on each other's heads.

As we sat together on his bed, a nurse came in to let us know it was almost time to go into surgery. "But first the anesthesiologist would like to speak to you." I felt my son's body tense up next to me, and I hugged him a little tighter.

A few minutes later, a totally unexpected answer to a child's desperate fear walked through the door. The anesthesiologist had a familiar face. It was Joey's dad! Joey was Jonathan's friend from his basketball team.

"Jonathan, what are you doing here?" he asked. Jonathan explained, and then admitted to being "a little afraid" of the impending surgery. Joey's dad smiled as he leaned in close and said, "Don't be afraid, Jonathan. I'm not going to leave your side for one minute. Okay, buddy? You're going to be all right!" At that, Jonathan's eyes lit up, and every trace of fear disappeared. The two continued to chatter nonstop about basketball until it was time to go into surgery.

"Bye, Mom, I'll see you later!" Jonathan waved. I blew him a kiss and smiled as I watched him go.

I walked down the corridor to the waiting area, my emotions surging within me. Once again, I had been humbled by the power of God's love. Not only had God spoken to us—an ordinary mother and child—through his sacred word, but he had also sent us a human, tangible sign of his never-faltering faithfulness. That day, "Do not be afraid, I am with you always" was etched into our hearts in an unforgettable way.

A pseudonym has been used at the author's request.

Bluebells and Blessings
By Jennifer Waroway
Winnipeg, Manitoba, Canada

O LORD of hosts,
happy is everyone who trusts in you. (Psalm 84:12)

My grandfather, Joseph, was a farmer. His days were long and filled with many chores. As a young child, I often spent warm summer days playing on the farm. I would search through the fields for small frogs and grasshoppers, exploring the earth for sweet berries, wild mushrooms, and four-leaf clover. When I wasn't coasting my bicycle down gravel roads, I enjoyed walking barefooted through the trees looking for wild flowers hidden within magical forests.

One afternoon, Grandpa offered me a ride on the old hay wagon that he was pulling with his antique John Deere tractor. I sat on the back of the weathered wood with my feet hanging over the edge so that I could feel the long prairie grasses tickling my toes. The wheels wobbled in and out of potholes, and the sides of the wagon gently swayed from side to side. I hung on to the planks to keep my balance.

As we approached the first bend, a patch of bluebells appeared. I gasped at the beauty of these tiny flowers—they were jewels in the pasture, sapphires scattered among tire ruts and cow pies. Grandpa stopped the tractor and stepped down from his perch to secure some plywood boards which had shifted in the wagon. I immediately jumped down and began collecting the fragile blossoms. The bluebells captivated me for some time, but eventually I lifted my head to see why Grandpa was not continuing on toward the barn. In complete wonder, I watched Grandpa stooping to gather his own bouquet of flowers. Then, with a kind smile, he extended the bluebells to me. I accepted them with a certain reverence.

I know I witnessed my grandfather's love that day. Until then, I had assumed that Grandpa was much too busy to be bothered with my silly childhood pursuits. With his farm spread out over hundreds of acres, I had imagined that his world was far removed from mine. Naively, I had believed that I was often alone in the wide-open spaces. Most likely, Grandpa knew all about my little "getaways" and watched out for me without my being aware of it.

This memory of my grandfather helped me during a difficult

period that came after I tried and failed to help a friend who was experiencing a prolonged spiritual and emotional struggle. Although it was difficult to balance a career, finances, family expectations, and other responsibilities, I had made an effort to support my friend in any way I could. I believed that if we prayed and asked God for healing, my friend's struggles would be resolved.

No matter what I did, however, my friend was not interested in being helped and often made comments that made *me* feel insecure. I was deeply hurt and angry that the time and effort I had invested seemed wasted. I was also angry with God for letting me down. I feared that this experience might be an indication that I was a failure. My hurt, anger, and fear began to separate me from God. Praying became extremely difficult. I lost any desire to reach out to others and felt almost completely disconnected from God. I was beginning to lose hope and felt very alone.

While I was thumbing through my Bible one evening, my eyes fell on Psalm 84, verse 12: "O LORD of hosts, happy is everyone who trusts in you." I began to meditate on the word "trust." Repeating this sacred word did not bring immediate comfort, but it did dissolve some of the pain in my heart. It was the beginning. Over time, I felt my spirit slowly rekindle through prayer and meditation.

Meditating on trust awakened my childhood memories about Grandpa. He was the one who taught me that even when you think you are alone, someone is always watching out for you. Of course, God is closer than Grandpa could ever be. No matter how discouraged I become, God is present as the Father, the Son, and the Holy Spirit.

When I humbly bow my head and accept that God cares for me as Grandpa did, then I can open my heart to receive the blessings he extends. I am able to witness his love in my life. God does not hand me a bouquet of bluebells to reveal his love—he blesses me with graces much more beautiful than flowers.

3

Wake-Up Calls

The stories in this chapter are about people who have had their eyes opened to some deeper aspect of God's call and presence in their lives. Whether through ordinary or extraordinary events, whether suddenly or over time, these men and women received clearer vision about such important realities as God's great mercy and love for them, their own deepest desires and needs, the healing power of repentance and forgiveness, and their unique place in God's plan.

From your own experience, you probably know that the Lord calls in many ways, for many purposes. Some of his calls lead to major life changes. Others provide the ongoing, daily-life help we all need. Are we sensitive to the Lord's voice and presence? Do we watch for him? Do we open ourselves to his Spirit? Our loving God calls us—much more often than we think!

Think About It!

Jesus walks among us today, calling us just as surely as he once called the people he met in Nazareth and Jerusalem. "Let us desire to know his voice," wrote Cardinal John Henry Newman. "Let us pray for the gift of watchful ears and a willing heart. He does not call all men in one way; he calls us each in his own way."

Pray It!

Talk to the Lord about your desire to hear him more clearly and more often, using this Scripture passage as your prayer starter:

> The one who enters by the gate is the shepherd of the sheep. The gatekeeper opens the gate for him, and the sheep hear his voice. He calls his own sheep by name and leads them out. When he has brought out all his own, he goes ahead of them, and the sheep follow him because they know his voice. They will not follow a stranger, but they will run from him because they do not know the voice of strangers. (John 10:2-5)

He Still Works Miracles

By Jeanne Legault

Ponteix, Saskatchewan, Canada

Bless the LORD, *O my soul, ... who heals all your diseases, who redeems your life from the Pit. (Psalm 103:2-4)*

I am from a family of fifteen children. My mother died while giving birth to the last child. At the time, my oldest sister, Marguerite, was married and expecting her first child; my youngest sibling was three; my twin brother and I were thirteen. It was a very difficult time for us all, but our father, being of strong faith, helped us to accept what had happened and move on with life.

One day nearly twenty-five years ago, as I was raising my own family, I noticed a hairpin-shaped lump near my left breast. A biopsy revealed that I had a very rare cancer. There were fewer than fifty cases in North America and only three in Canada, my doctor told me, and nobody who had it had ever lived longer than two years.

"I'm going to take this one day at a time," was my first reaction. But when I got home, the gravity of the situation blew my mind.

A few weeks later, I had surgery so that the doctors could take more tissue samples. The tests confirmed the original diagnosis, and so five doctors met to assess how to proceed. The hours spent waiting for the doctors' report were agonizing. Finally, a decision was made to send my tissue sample and X rays for further analysis at a hospital in the United States and to have me begin very aggressive chemotherapy treatments.

During this entire time, I was trying to place myself completely in God's hands. What helped me was that five years earlier, I had been baptized in the Spirit at a charismatic renewal conference and had sensed the Lord showing me that I would someday be going back and forth to doctors. I was strengthened by this knowledge and by the fact that many people were praying for me—my family and friends, members of my prayer group, and even the doctor's wife, who gave me a little angel statue.

Somehow I was able to tell the Lord that I wanted only his will and nothing else. This wasn't always easy—I had five children, the youngest was only eight years old. Still, I was convinced that no matter what happened, God would take good care of them, just as he had done for our family when my mother died in 1949.

Six months went by. "We're still waiting for the results," my doctor kept telling me whenever I inquired. It was another exercise in trust and patient endurance. When the phone call finally came, it brought truly amazing news: the specialists at the U.S. hospital had not been able to find any trace of the cancer. It had simply disappeared!

"You've been healed," my doctor told me. Some time later, he showed my X rays to a pathologist friend of his from another city. That doctor looked at the X rays, noticed the date on them, and said I must be "dead and gone." No, my doctor assured him, I was very much alive and well. "Then tell her she's been healed," said the pathologist. "There's no other explanation."

Bless the LORD, O my soul,
and do not forget all his benefits—
who forgives all your iniquity,
who heals all your diseases,
who redeems your life from the Pit,
who crowns you with steadfast love and mercy.
(Psalm 103:2-4)

These verses, which were shared with me by a nun in our prayer group, have become very meaningful to me. They carry a message about our gracious God who loves us so much that he gave his only Son so that we might be made whole.

Why did this merciful God heal my disease and save my life? Not because of anything I did, I'm sure. Without having all the answers, I believe that the prayers of my faith community played an important part. I also believe that I was healed for the benefit of other people, who need to know that God is still performing miracles.

Imagine how many healings we might see if we prayed for our family members and friends more often! Let's put our faith in God, then, and ask him to open our eyes to "*all* his benefits."

The First Day of My Life of Faith
By Anthony Cassano*

When it was evening on that day, the first day of the week, and the doors of the house where the disciples had met were locked for fear of the Jews, Jesus came and stood among them and said, "Peace be with you." (John 20:19)

The young couple who were in charge of the house had been married only a year or two. He worked as a paramedic, she at a bank. One of my new housemates was in medical school. Another was a college student majoring in an obscure foreign language; a third was a medical technician; a fourth had left high school early, picked up occasional jobs, and spent a fair amount of time tinkering with his motorcycle in the garage.

These were the people who lived in the "guest house." It seemed that the six of them would have had barely enough in common for a conversation. Yet here they were, living together in order to provide hospitality for people like me, who had come to visit the newly founded lay Christian community to which they belonged.

The amazing thing about my hosts was not only that they got along with each other; there was an indefinable something they seemed to share that made the whole arrangement feel natural. Their somewhat helter-skelter life together could have made their rented house feel as empty as many another transient campus-area living situation. Yet it felt like a home.

While I puzzled over this, I noticed something else surprising about my hosts: they talked about Jesus. Now I had recently left a college situation where my friends and I had taken theology courses and had gotten into many deep discussions. So I was not a stranger to "Jesus-talk." But the conversations of my guest house friends were different. They talked about Jesus as someone who played an important role in their lives. They talked about him as someone they had met. This floored me.

I was full of doubts about God. My hosts were perhaps not able to engage in a discussion of my theological problems, but they offered something that seemed to make an end run around my doubts. It was as though they said, "We can't answer many of your questions about God's existence, but we can tell you about how he came into our lives and changed us."

A few days of living at the guest house provided me with plenty of opportunities for reflection.

Every afternoon the household gathered in the living room to pray for twenty minutes before dinner. I would join them, not praying myself (I didn't believe there was anyone to pray to), but listening with interest.

My visit happened to occur just after Easter, and so the tag line (the "antiphon") at the beginning and end of their prayers came from a gospel verse having to do with Jesus' resurrection. It was taken from an account in the Gospel of John (20:19) in which Jesus appeared to his disciples on the evening of the day of his resurrection. "When it was evening on that day, the first day of the week, and the doors of the house where the disciples had met were locked for fear of the Jews, Jesus came and stood among them and said, 'Peace be with you.'"

I sat through afternoon prayers for several days as a neutral observer. And then one afternoon it struck me: *this* afternoon, in *this* house, in *this* motley group being gathered together in *this* living room, the same event is repeating itself. Jesus is here.

It would be simplifying things too much to say that this single insight resolved all my doubts about God, but it was a moment of real grace. It helped me see what—or I should say *who*—was the elusive something that I sensed in the life these guest house members shared together.

Along with some other moments of grace, this one in the living room helped me take what at the time seemed an almost absurd step: to turn toward the darkness and silence and say to God, "If you are here, if you are the Father, then my life really belongs to you."

That was the beginning of my life of faith.

Since that time, years ago, the verse of John's Gospel has always shone with a special light for me. It reminds me that here and now, wherever I happen to be, Jesus, who has conquered death, makes himself present and brings his peace.

A pseudonym has been used at the author's request.

Asleep No More

By Katherine Murphy
Clifton Park, New York

Awake, O sleeper, and arise from the dead, and Christ shall give
you light. (Ephesians 5:14)

Fifteen years ago, I was diagnosed with cancer. I was thirty-nine at the time, married, the mother of two young boys, and a schoolteacher. I had been in excellent health and was experiencing no symptoms when the cancer was discovered at my annual checkup. I was scared.

Caught up in the turmoil of doctors' appointments, second opinions, and treatments, I began to pray. "God, help me. Let the doctors know what they're doing. Please don't let me die." This was all I could manage—not only was I out of practice with prayer, but I had never been in touch with Scripture.

Growing up, I had parents who had strong faith. I attended parochial schools and prayed as a young girl. But during my teenage years, I became preoccupied and began to drift away from God. By the time I was an adult, God and religion had faded into the background. I fulfilled my Sunday obligation to attend Mass and thought that was enough to define me as a Catholic. With the onset of cancer, I knew it wasn't. I needed help and began to search for the God I had known in my childhood.

A few weeks after my diagnosis, a friend told me about a seminar at my church. "It's for anyone who wants to draw closer to God," she said. That was me. I wanted God to come into my life and save me from cancer. At the seminar, the leaders encouraged us to spend time each day praying and reading the Bible. I felt clumsy praying and resisted the formal prayers I had grown up with. Mostly I continued to ask for things.

But reading Scripture was something new. Once before, for a college theology course on "Human Suffering in Literature," I had read the New Testament. Though I had seen it as a true depiction of the human condition some two thousand years ago, I considered it just another piece of literature—something completely removed from my life in the twentieth century. This time, as I read at random in the New Testament and the psalms, I had an entirely different reaction to the Bible. It struck me that people today and people long ago both experience the same suffering and search for meaning. I saw that the psalms can apply to anyone at anytime. Many stories in the Bible—including those I had half-heard at Sunday Mass—suddenly became living and relevant. But it was when I read St. Paul's Letter to the Ephesians that the words leaped off the page at me: "Awake, O sleeper, and arise from the dead, and Christ shall give you light" (5:14).

That was it! Being asleep seemed the perfect metaphor for my relationship with God. His love was all around me—made concrete in the goodness of many people who had been extending themselves and reaching out to me—but I had never noticed it before. For the first time, I was waking up and becoming aware of God's presence in others. The words from Ephesians haunted me for days.

Soon afterward my husband encouraged me to attend a luncheon sponsored by his business group. He thought it would interest me and get me out of the funk of my treatments. I didn't want to go, but I couldn't say no to Eva, the secretary from the main office. Though I didn't know her well, she had supported me throughout my illness with flowers, notes, holiday cards, and post-treatment phone calls, touching me each time with her kindness. At Eva's urging, I attended the luncheon.

As I sat there talking with Eva, I noticed right away that something was different. What was it? *It's me!* I finally realized. I was more aware. I was listening better, connecting in a way I hadn't before. Conversations seemed more real. *Have I really been so self-absorbed?* I wondered. *Have I been only half-listening to what people have been saying to me?* I felt as though I had been sitting behind a curtain hearing muffled voices.

The contrast jolted me. What was happening? Was cancer opening my eyes to other people? Was it opening my ears as well? Then I remembered: "Awake, O sleeper, and arise from the dead, and Christ shall give you light." Yes, cancer was waking me up. And the words from Ephesians were waking me up to God's goodness around me.

Many years have passed since then, and thanks to God I remain cancer free. Yet I am grateful for the opportunity that my illness provided, because without it I might not have turned to God. My prayer life has grown. I continue to read Scripture and to be touched by God's word.

However, the words from Ephesians still speak loudly, especially when I feel distant from God or find myself slipping into my old ways. They speak when I am "too busy" to pray more or to pick up my Bible. When I hear them now, I realize that I am not paying attention to God's presence around me. And I know that the remedy is simple. All I need to do is turn to God, who is always ready to awaken sleepers to the good news of his peace, grace, and love.

Keep the Light On
By John Karcher
McLeansboro, Illinois

But I tell you that on the day of judgment it will be more tolerable for the land of Sodom than for you. (Matthew 11:24)

Four years ago, at the age of thirty-four, I was feeling like I had reached the pinnacle of life. I had a beautiful wife, two stepchildren and a younger daughter, a nice home and car, a good job, and no financial worries. "This is as good as it gets," I told myself. But I wasn't completely satisfied. Deep down, I knew there must be more.

At work my boss was experiencing a religious conversion. I heard stories about what he had been like, and I was fascinated by the changes in him. At some point, I found myself praying, or perhaps just thinking, "I want what he has."

Then one night not long afterward, I had an unusual experience. I woke up at 3:15 a.m. and got up to use the bathroom. (That's how I know I wasn't dreaming.) Upon returning to bed, I saw something like a giant movie screen with a beautiful sunrise on it. I had a mental impression of a voice behind me saying, "This is me." Then I saw total darkness, and the voice said, "This is not me." The very next moment, I seemed to be in a huge ballroom with a beautiful shiny chandelier. Once again the voice said, "This is me." Then a light switch was turned off, and again there was darkness and the words, "This is not me." As the switch was flipped back on, the voice said, "Keep the light on." Into my head popped a Scripture reference: Matthew 11:24. Feeling puzzled but very peaceful, I went back to bed.

The next morning I woke up and remembered the Scripture reference. Now, I really didn't know my Bible verses. I always followed along during the Mass readings, but sitting at home reading Scripture was something I never did. In fact, the only Bible I could remember seeing when I was growing up was a large family version that I had thought was too holy to touch.

Since I didn't have a Bible of my own, I asked my boss to look up Matthew 11:24. What a slap in the face it was to read: "I tell you that on the day of judgment it will be more tolerable for the land of Sodom than for you"! Here I was, a cradle Catholic from a good family—someone who had probably missed weekend Mass only fifteen times in his life and who even gave a few dollars occasionally to help the church. What could this verse possibly have to do with me?

It wasn't long before I bought myself a Bible. Another Scripture verse came to me within the next month: Revelation 3:16. I looked it up and found another sobering word: "So, because you are lukewarm, and neither cold nor hot, I am about to spit you out of my mouth." Talk about revelation coming to a person! God was showing me that I was basically a pew-sitter, putting in my hour a week at church and then going back to my usual life. Somehow, I didn't feel condemned or discouraged by this knowledge. Instead, it gave me a deep urge to actually know God.

At the suggestion of my boss, I started to learn about the Holy Spirit. I had heard about the Spirit many times before, but this was different. Finally one day, I asked my boss to pray with me. As he asked the Spirit to come into my life in a deeper way, I felt a warmth go through my body and had a profound sense of God's love.

How can I describe my experience of the Spirit's action? It is as if my life is a chest of drawers and the Holy Spirit is helping me do some housecleaning. Together we pull out one drawer, dump it out, and get rid of the things that don't fit or are out of style. He helps me straighten the drawer up, and then we close it and start another drawer. If I go back and mess up the drawer a little, the Holy Spirit gently shows me how to put things back in order again. He helps me in so many ways, teaching me how to be a good husband, father, and spiritual leader of my family—and especially, leading me to Jesus.

I came to know Jesus personally once I got started reading my Bible. At first I would complain to God that I just didn't have the time. I'd get up, go to work, come home and do a few things around the house, spend time with my family, and never get to my Bible. Then three mornings in a row, I woke up at 5:00 a.m. and was unable to go back to sleep. Finally getting the hint, I got up, grabbed my Bible and *The Word Among Us,* and started reading.

Jesus has come alive to me through this time of meditation, prayer, and reading the day's Bible passages. My relationship with him has changed everything. Now I'm only too eager to "keep the light on" by meeting him at the beginning of each new day.

Four Angels of Mercy
By Maggie Barrick
Baltimore, Maryland

You are not your own; you were bought with a price. So glorify God in your body. (1 Corinthians 6:19-20)

One Tuesday night in September, I left a restaurant after having dinner with a friend. As I was driving home, I noticed an open-bed truck in front of me. It was full of wood and other materials. Suddenly, something flew out of the back of the vehicle. It rolled under my Nissan pickup and lodged itself under the front of the engine so that I was dragging it along with me. The driver of the truck was oblivious to what had happened and continued on his way.

On my right, a gray-haired woman in a silver car shouted for me to roll down my window. "There's something stuck under your truck!" she yelled. I mouthed that I knew it and was trying to get off the road. It was impossible to do this right away, however, because there was traffic on both sides of me. Finally, I was able to pull into a shopping center parking lot. The lady in the silver car pulled in behind me, and as I got out of my truck, three men appeared.

One of the men retrieved a long stick from his vehicle and dislodged the object from underneath my truck. It turned out to be a ten-gallon gasoline can. How much gasoline was in it, I don't know—but the can was smoldering. Our mouths dropped open as we realized what could have happened. "You're lucky that can didn't ignite," said one of the men. "Your truck could have gone up in flames." Two of the men disposed of the hot, smashed can, and then everyone went on their way.

While I was driving home, it hit me forcefully that I had been rescued from a very dangerous situation. Through the grace of God, I had been spared. God had sent help in the form of four complete strangers who realized I was in trouble and cared enough to make sure I would be okay. And my pickup had not even been damaged at all!

I was at a loss for words to express the emotions I was feeling. But as one thought kept going through my mind, over and over again, I heard myself saying, "He owns you." That night I got down on my knees, said the *Our Father*, and completely surrendered my life to God's will. Now, more clearly than ever, I know that God loves me and has a plan for me—a *great* plan!

A Week with the Word
By Ria Coppens
Bright Grove, Ontario, Canada

A Samaritan woman came to draw water, and Jesus said to her, "Give me a drink." (John 4:7)

One September Sunday, after two years of making excuses to avoid the moment, there I finally was—arriving at a retreat house for a week of directed meditation on Scripture. The doubts and fears came rushing in. *What am I doing here? I'm a very active person. How can I pray for a whole week?* But it was too late to go back on my decision, so I resolved to make the best of it. That evening, we were told to reflect on Psalm 139 and Isaiah 55, let go of mental clutter, and relax. It was a promising start.

The next morning, in a private meeting with the retreat director, Fr. Mike, I was given four other readings to meditate on for forty-five minutes each. It became a very easy and peaceful day. I felt relaxed and happy to be away from the distractions of normal living. On day two, Fr. Mike shattered my peaceful mood and shocked me by asking why I was angry. Of course, I denied feeling angry at all! As he spoke, though, I slowly began to see areas of my life where my hurt and anger resonated. He sent me to the chapel to ponder two questions:

What is there in my life that I resent?
What would I do differently if I were God?

I believe this was the first time in my life that I looked deeply into my soul and was very honest—with myself, but above all with God. My reflection time became a powerful first-time dialogue with God. It was the beginning of a big change in my life.

The next day Fr. Mike told me to read Job 38-40, which I had never meditated on before. As I considered Job's own dialogue with God, I felt similarly addressed. "Who do you think you are, that you know all the answers?" was one of the questions the Lord asked me. I started to realize that I did not let God do in me what he wanted to do.

On Wednesday, I was directed to look at Christ's judgment of the "sheep" and the "goats" (Matthew 25:31-46). In this gospel, I saw something of what the Lord wanted from me and of how I was not responding. The message was so powerful that even now when I read this passage, I still hear what the Lord was saying. Again Fr. Mike left me with a question: "What is the Lord inviting you to do at this time in your life?"

As important and powerful as these first three days were, it was Thursday's meditation—on John 4:1-42—that turned my whole life around. This is the day I will never forget. By this time, I no longer felt tense or frightened. As I grew in knowledge of myself, with all my flaws and failures, I was also getting to know God's love and patience with me.

Heading outside to meditate in the sunshine, I passed by the chapel. Something drew me in. No one else was there, so I heeded my instinct to remain and began reading John 4. Something powerful happened to me when I reached verse 7. Somehow, I heard not only Jesus' request to the Samaritan woman—"Give me a drink"—but also one of his very last words: "I am thirsty" (John 19:28). Then in my mind, I suddenly saw Jesus on the cross, asking *me* for a drink. More clearly, I also saw how I had been refusing to give him the drink he desired from me.

For various reasons, I had given up all involvement in my parish some time before. This was what the Lord wanted, I thought. Fr. Mike had put his finger on my anger and unhappiness—signs that I was not walking in God's way of peace and joy. Job 38, too, had shown me that I was misinterpreting the situation. But it was Jesus' invitation that brought healing and transformation. "I am thirsty. Give me a drink." My tears flowed, and I stayed in the chapel for a long time. I promised Jesus that I would deny him no longer. I went back to my room exhausted and spent a sleepless night. As I told Fr. Mike the next morning, I had no idea how to change my circumstances. He said to take a day off. "Go and sit by the river. Relax and wait for what the Lord wants you to see." It became a day of resting in God, of saying, "Here I am, Lord. I have come to do your will." At the end of it, I still had no specific answers about how to change my life, but I knew I could trust God to lead me. At the Eucharist that day, I gave the Lord my formal "yes" to whatever he had in mind. I have never looked back.

It has been seventeen years since that experience, and it is as vivid now as it was then. Today I express my "yes" to God by making home and hospital visits to the sick members of our parish and by visiting a nursing home once a week. I have found ways to keep praying and reflecting on Scripture. Four years ago, I started a small sharing group. We meet every other week to read and contemplate God's word together and share insights from our other spiritual reading. I belong to a small contemplative prayer group and also meet weekly with a friend for mutual encouragement to more faithful prayer and action.

Though the journey is not always easy and I still have a long way to go, I have found deep joy and peace in giving the Lord what he wants from me. And no wonder. As I give Jesus a drink, he refreshes me with the "living water" that springs up to eternal life (John 4:10, 15). I thank God for our deeper relationship and for the privilege of serving him.

The Word That Turned My Life Around

By Michael Iwuchukwu
Obosi, Nigeria

He has anointed me to bring good news to the poor. He has sent me to proclaim release to the captives and recovery of sight to the blind, to let the oppressed go free. (Luke 4:18)

I was baptized and raised Catholic, but when I was fourteen, my life took a very wrong turn. I dropped out of school, went off to the city, and got in with a bad crowd. Very quickly, I learned to smoke and drink, and I lived an immoral lifestyle. I spent the next few years in total darkness, living with friends and managing my own little business.

One weekend several years ago, I went to visit my brother and his family. I had been planning to travel back to my house on Saturday, but it got too late. I spent the night at my brother's and then accompanied him to 6:00 a.m. Mass—but only because I didn't want him to find out that I no longer went to church. I certainly didn't want him interrogating me about my lifestyle! At the end of Mass, the priest introduced two missionaries from Canada and said that they had come to launch "Couples for Christ," a family renewal movement in the parish. They were beginning with a seven-day program, which was scheduled to start that very day.

Mainly because I was intrigued by these white missionaries, I decided to prolong my stay and attend the evening orientation session. I don't know what I was expecting, but something extraordinary happened to me when Luke 4:18 was read aloud and explained by the mission team leader. During his teaching about the types of people mentioned by our Lord in those verses—the "poor," the "captive," the "blind," and the "oppressed"—it dawned on me that I myself belonged to those four categories. And as the speaker went on to talk about God's love, I realized that our merciful God was reaching out to *me* personally! I suddenly understood that Jesus had come into the world out of love for me and that he greatly desired to set me free from bondage and reconcile me to the Father.

By the end of that session, I found myself in the shoes of the prodigal son and was ready to repent of my old way of life. Afterward, feeling lighter, I vowed to attend the remaining eleven talks. I did so by the grace of God. Then, in a special service led by one of the priests, I dedicated myself completely to God. Small weekly meetings with other people in this renewal movement provided further spiritual support, and I took them very seriously.

Now, almost four years later, the transforming power of the Holy Spirit continues to purify and cleanse me. I help to lead a "Singles for Christ" ministry in my own parish—and I hope that people around me can feel the radiating light of the Holy Spirit at work! Every day I thank God for my new life, and I pray that his word will break into the hearts of everyone who lives as I once did, so that they can join me in testifying to the goodness of our loving God.

4

Learning About God's Love

God loves you. We've seen this message written so many times that it can almost become a cliché, and yet the message is ever new, ever awesome. The Creator of heaven and earth really does love us, his creatures! And not only does he love us, he wants us to *experience* this love and to receive it for ourselves and for the benefit of our world.

As you read about the ways in which the contributors to this chapter came to a deeper understanding of God's love, ask the Holy Spirit to give you a fresh awareness of that love, too. Ask him to help you become a messenger of divine love. You won't be refused, for these are prayers after the heart of a God who *is* love (1 John 4:8).

Think About It!

One evening when Dorothy Day was lonely and far from home, a sudden and unexpected thought came to her—"of my importance as a daughter of God, daughter of a King." Of that moment, she wrote: "I felt a sureness of God's love.... God so loved me that he gave his only begotten Son. 'If a mother will forget her children, never will I forget thee' [John 3:16; Isaiah 49:15]. Such tenderness. And with such complete ingratitude we forget the Father and his love!" (*On Pilgrimage*).

Pray It!

The human mind just can't conceive the magnitude of God's love. Still, that didn't stop St. Paul from praying that we might all understand it. Use his prayer as a guide to your own:

I pray that you may have the power to comprehend, with all the saints, what is the breadth and length and height and depth, and to know the love of Christ that surpasses knowledge, so that you may be filled with all the fullness of God. (Ephesians 3:18-19)

Like a Child
By Aline Rousseau-Zunti
Lloydminster, Alberta, Canada

Unless you change and become like children, you will never enter the kingdom of heaven. (Matthew 18:3)

My twin sister and I are the oldest in a family of thirteen children. We were raised in the 1930s in a very Catholic home in rural Saskatchewan. Evening prayer was a year-round must for us, with special recitation of the rosary during Advent, Lent, and the months of May and October. Even so, we were never a close-knit family. For my part, I often felt guilty because I didn't love my father. I didn't think he was lovable. When I grew up, I realized he was an alcoholic.

When Dad grew old and I realized that he would not be with us much longer, I wrote him a letter. Dad had never learned to read, so my husband and I made a special trip to the senior home where he was living to read it to him. In the letter, I asked him to forgive me for not always having been the loving daughter I should have been. I told him that I forgave him with all my heart for the hurts he had caused me. My father listened attentively, and when I finished he said, *"C'est beau,"* which is French for "That's nice." We left, and I praised God for giving me that peace which is indescribable.

A few months later, we got a phone call that Dad had suffered a stroke. We packed our things and left for the hospital. When we got to my father's bedside, I was thoroughly disgusted. Here he was, on the brink of death, and all he could talk about was getting a jug of wine and having a party. I started praying silently, and I noticed that he really settled down whenever I did this. But whenever someone would come into the room, he'd get all agitated again.

When I couldn't sleep that night, I prayed. I was really feeling down. "Does he really have to end his days in this state of mind?" I asked God.

My aunt stayed with Dad in the hospital all night, and early the next morning we arrived to relieve her and to feed him breakfast. Now he was down in the dumps. "I'm just a good-for-nothing old man. You have to feed me like a baby. I'm just good for nothing...." He went on and on. At noon my sister Marguerite fed him; then my daughter Evelyne, who is a registered nurse, shaved him. All Dad did was complain and complain. When suppertime came, he continued his lament—he was good for nothing and would die good for nothing.

Finally I had an inspiration. "Dad, do you want to go to heaven?" I asked. He looked at me quite surprised.

"Well, eh, yes, I want to go to heaven. What do you think? I sure don't want to go to hell!"

"Well then," I said firmly but as lovingly as I could. "Jesus said in the Bible: 'Unless you change and become like children, you will never enter the kingdom of heaven.' So there you go. Thank God that we can take care of you like a little child, because that's what he wants of you now."

"I never thought of that," Dad said quietly. He became very pensive. There was silence—a heavenly silence.

I can't begin to tell you how this "word of the Lord" changed my Dad! For the first time in our lives, he began telling me and my sister how good we were to take care of him so well. There was not one more complaint, but only thanksgiving for every little act of goodness we did for him! I had never *ever* heard my father say that any of us children had done anything good—there was always something that could have been done differently or better. What a transformation!

On the last day of my father's life, I spent all morning with him.

He enjoyed it, and so did I. In fact, I had never enjoyed Dad's company like this before. We talked about heaven and about a dream he had about my mother, who had died almost thirty years before. She had come to meet him at the end of a field and asked him why he had taken so long to come join her. That morning, it seemed like heaven was very close.

At noon I fed Dad his lunch. He was having a very hard time swallowing, but he never gave up. "Is it good?" I asked when he was halfway through his corn soup. "It sure is," he said. I fed him every drop of the soup and followed it up with some ice cream. And again he said the words that sounded so heavenly to me: "You are so good to take care of me like this!" That evening, as he was being prepared for his evening meal, my father died—gently, quietly, and peacefully.

But it wasn't only my father who was able to "change and become like children" during those final days. His transformation freed me to relate to him with love, as a child normally would. Now I can say that I learned to love my dad before he died. How I praise God for that!

Speak to Me, Lord!
By Anne Costa
Baldwinsville, New York

I am with you always. (Matthew 28:20)

Each of us has a cross to bear. Mine has been to experience periodic bouts of depression. These are times of great interior darkness when I am not certain that Christ's light will ever penetrate the cloud of despair that enshrouds my soul. While I know in my head that I am never alone during these episodes, my heart often aches with loneliness as I experience a profound sense of disconnection from others and from God.

As a wife and the mother of a young child, I have had to learn how to "push through" these difficult times. Calling upon the grace of God, I labor intensely to complete the simplest tasks of my daily routine. Though I may not experience the consolation of God's presence, I am nonetheless grateful to get through the day, even if I am less charitable than I would like. The fact remains: I have to function, regardless of how I feel, because my family needs and depends on me to care for them.

The effort often takes every ounce of strength I can muster, leaving precious little energy for prayer and full participation in the sacraments. Nonetheless, I have a steadfast rule that holds firm even during times of deepest darkness: Go to church no matter what, no matter how bad you feel. Sometimes I am completely distracted and miss most of what is going on. Sometimes I sit in the farthest corner of the church and simply let the tears flow. Yet I try never to miss daily Mass during these times of depression (and I stay very near to the Sacrament of Reconciliation as well).

One morning at Mass, in the midst of a depressive episode, I cried out to Jesus from the depths of my heart. "*Where are you?*" It was an anguished plea of desperation, but it was also a turning point. I poured out my whole being in this interior prayer. I boldly asked Jesus to speak directly to me. I wanted an undeniable sign that he was still with me in my pain. "I need to know that you still love me," I told him in no uncertain terms. I released the prayer, imagining it as incense rising up to heaven before the face of God.

The next evening, as I was helping my five-year-old daughter settle down for the night, I felt particularly challenged by the late hour and my dragging spirit. It took some effort to drag myself back into her room when she called out emphatically, "Mommy, I need to tell you something." Then she said, "Mommy, sometimes I can't feel in my heart the love that you give me." Taken aback, I asked her to explain. "Sometimes, my heart doesn't feel happy and joyful," she said. "I know you love me, but I don't feel it in my heart."

I silently tossed up to Jesus the most effective prayer I know—"*Help!*"—and somehow, he gave me the right words. I told my daughter that feelings were just feelings and that they were okay to have, but that they didn't always match up with what was true. "The most important thing to remember is that I always love you, and Jesus always loves you—even when you can't feel it in your heart."

This satisfied her. She threw her arms around me and hugged me, exclaiming, "I feel so much better now!"

The next morning I woke up well before dawn, noticing a lightness in my heart that I hadn't felt in weeks. As I reflected on the previous night's conversation, a familiar voice spoke quietly to my heart. "Did you hear what you said last night? I gave you those words, because they are the words I speak to you." In that moment, I understood that Jesus had heard my prayer. I knew beyond a shadow of a doubt that he had never left me and that, even though I can't always feel it, he always loves me. There it was: the sign I had asked for, my unmistakable assurance. It was the undeniable voice of Jesus, speaking through one of his littlest instruments to assure me that "I am with you always."

A Place in God's Family
By Grace*

Even if my father and mother forsake me,
the LORD will take me in. (Psalm 27:10, NAB)

Though I don't have many memories from early childhood, I do recall that my three brothers and I once had a two-parent home. Then, for reasons that I was too young to understand, there came a point when we were no longer a family.

My mother tried to raise us on her own, but her mind was unbalanced. My three brothers and I wandered the streets of Pittsburgh with her day and night. I always thought we were lost because we were forever walking and walking but never getting to a destination. One place where we lived had no furniture. Often we had no food. If we did get some, my mother did strange things—she might peel an orange, give us the rind, and throw away the fruit. We slept on newspapers, and my brothers and I often played with pictures we cut out, especially pictures of refrigerators filled with food.

One day I found myself in a shelter for children. My mother had threatened to kill us if the police refused to take us. I was separated from my brothers. Scared, alone, and confused that my mother could have abandoned us, I lay in bed looking out on a dark, star-filled sky. With tears streaming down my face, I cried out, "God, please take care of me because I have no one." I cried myself to sleep that night, but I believe God's angels were with me in that room.

After several months in the shelter, I was placed in a foster home. Once again, I was confused and scared. No one explained what was happening or why I was being moved. I spent the next thirteen years there, but I didn't feel that I belonged. My foster parents gave me the basic food, shelter, and clothing, but they did not accept me into their family. I was never told that I was loved; I was never hugged, comforted, or encouraged. Though I had many blood relatives, none of them claimed me or even tried to contact me. It was as if I had never existed.

All these experiences led to very unhealthy patterns of thought. I reasoned that since no one loved or wanted me—not even my own mother—there must be something wrong with me. I had deep feelings of rejection and worthlessness. I never discussed these with anyone, but over the years I became bitter, angry, defensive, and resentful. I built high, thick walls and did not allow anyone to break through them.

Since I had been baptized Catholic, I went to Sunday Mass and even to a Catholic grade school during these difficult years. But the only time I experienced God and was at peace was when I was asleep. When things got too hard to bear, I would escape into a dream world where I did not have to deal with the pressures of my life. I believe that God used this to give me a temporary escape. When I dreamt, God comforted me and I awoke refreshed. It was a strength I could count on.

Eventually, I fell away from the Church. I married a wonderful man and had two beautiful children, but my life was still not right. I continued to hold on to the past without ever talking about it. This produced inner tensions that led to my first adult encounter with the Lord. One day, very arrogantly, I told him, "Lord, I'm not doing very well managing my life. If you think you can do better, it's yours. Come into my life and fix it."

That instant, something happened, and I knew it. Things began to change. I returned to church and went to Mass every week. I had a great desire to know the Lord. The problem was that I had no desire to know or love his creation, his people. I simply had no use for them. Despite these feelings, I became active in different ministries in the church.

One afternoon five years later, instead of going to confession in a different parish, as I usually did, I went to my own church. The priest knew me only from seeing me at Mass, and I thought it would be a simple matter of receiving absolution and going on my way.

But it didn't take Father long to figure out that I had been through some hard times. In fact, he bluntly interrupted me. "Something happened to you," he said. My eyes opened wide in surprise. Stunned and scared, I did not know how to respond. "Yes, something did happen," I replied. And then I shut down and refused to discuss it.

Father did not force the issue or badger me, but he encouraged me to talk and said I could call him whenever I was ready. I went home upset and angry and complained to the Lord that "he had no right to bring up the past!" Then I felt this peaceful, calm voice telling me, "Listen to him. I want to heal you." Well, I didn't like that either. "I don't need healing!" was my response. "I just want to be left alone."

Eventually I did go and talk to Father—not once, but many times. It was not easy. At first I did not know how to express myself. I had to learn to trust this priest, especially when he told me that God was preparing me for something and that I had to let go of my anger. It made me angry that I didn't know how to do that! I spent many hours before the Blessed Sacrament and in Father's office. The point of my healing came when I accepted the past as over and done with, and went on to truly forgive—from deep within my heart—the many people whom I felt had wronged me. Finally, I was able to ask forgiveness for having harbored so much anger and resentment. That moment when I accepted God's gift of healing, I was in ecstasy!

Little by little, I began opening up to people and allowing them to love me. As I did, I discovered that Father was right. God did indeed prepare me for something—for passing on his love to the many special people he puts into my life.

I now work for hospice, caring for the terminally ill. It was a hospice patient who was the first person the Lord put in my path for me to love and be loved by. He was a dear man who was dying of cancer. I often held his hand when the pain got too much for him. He was a spiritual person, and I was honored to walk with him on his journey home to God. He passed away knowing that I loved him, and I knew myself what it truly means to love and be loved.

As I have reflected on my life, with all its confusion and heartache, Psalm 27:10 has come alive for me: "Even if my father and mother forsake me, the LORD will take me in." God's words have been realized in my life. God has brought me into his family, where there is peace, love, and acceptance. I would not trade it for anything.

At the author's request, a pseudonym has been used.

Am I Worth It?
By Dave Steeples
Morton, Illinois

You did not choose me, but I chose you. (John 15:16)

The first time God's word came to life for me was during a retreat weekend sponsored by Cursillo, an international Catholic renewal movement. As a cradle Catholic, I had heard all the Bible stories of God's love for us. At the weekend, I *saw* this love in action and realized that I did not have it in my heart.

I was especially struck by the way the Cursillo community showed us the love that is God. I saw it in the Cursillo members who gave the retreat and came to cook and serve the meals. I felt it in the prayers of many other members who were interceding for the weekend.

One night, during a session held in St. Mary's Cathedral in Peoria, Illinois, we were invited to meditate on what the weekend had meant to us so far. As I thought about all the loving effort that had gone into it—the talks, the meals, the prayers and fasting being offered for us from Cursillo centers all around the world—I felt quite overwhelmed. I looked at the painting of the crucified Jesus that was hanging over the altar. Here was the ultimate expression of God's love. I put my head down and prayed, "Am I worth it? Is my soul worth the price that Jesus paid? Am I even worth all that is being done for me this weekend?" Then I heard that still, small voice say, "You haven't chosen me, I have chosen you" (John 15: 16).

My response to that voice welled up from deep within me: "My Lord and my God." As I thought about God's love for me, I experienced it in the deepest part of my soul.

After the weekend, the first thing I did was to buy a Bible and start reading it daily. Since I wanted to help other people know God's love and come into a deep personal relationship with Jesus, I applied to be on a Cursillo team. One day I got a phone call from a man who was leading a team into a state prison. I had never really thought about doing prison ministry, but I said I would pray about his invitation to join. Picking up my Bible, I read 1 Corinthians 12:4-7, where St. Paul says that the Spirit distributes various gifts and services, giving each member of the church "the manifestation of the Spirit for the common good." I called back the next day and said yes.

That was thirteen years ago. During this time I have grown in my faith and love for both Jesus and his word. I have served on twelve different Cursillo teams so far.

Two years ago, our pastor called to ask whether I was open to the possibility of becoming a permanent deacon. Feeling both honored and quite humbled, I told him that my wife Lorie and I would gladly come to an informational and discernment meeting with him and a representative from the Office for the Diaconate. Should I have been surprised when, during the meeting, Fr. Mark read aloud this Scripture verse: "You did not choose me, but I chose you"?

We made our decision and are now in the "aspirancy year" of the diaconate program—the first of four years of formation. I can only praise the Lord for his goodness!

A Title for Grandma
By Cecilia Martin
Modoc, Indiana

O LORD, you have searched me and known me.
You know when I sit down and when I rise up;
you discern my thoughts from far away.
(Psalm 139:1-2)

When my grandchildren were very young, they started calling me "own Grandma." I thought this was quite unusual but accepted it without question as their way of distinguishing me from their other grandmothers.

One day while my son David and his children were visiting with me, my granddaughter Kristen addressed me using this title. David said, "Kristen, tell Grandma why she is 'own Grandma.'" Kristen looked puzzled. My son turned to Bryant and asked the same question. Bryant, being the oldest, replied in the matter-of-fact tone children use when explaining the obvious to their parents: "Because she is my own Grandma."

David persisted and asked Bryant, "But do you remember why she is your 'own' Grandma?" Then David answered the question himself: "It's because your other grandmas have lots of grandchildren, but this one only has you and Kristen, and now your brother Andrew, for grandchildren. So she is your very own, because no one else has her for a grandma." The children smiled and said, "That's right, Dad," as if he had finally figured out what they knew all along.

Genuinely touched at discovering the thought process behind my title, I pondered this subject of "own grandma" one morning while I was meditating. I had just read Psalm 139, which speaks of God's intimate knowledge of each one of us. As I started thinking about God and how I pray and petition him, it suddenly struck me that I think of him in the same way my grandchildren think of me—as my "own God."

Although God's children are many and he is but one God, I know that when I pray I have his exclusive attention. God knows me. He and I have a one-to-one relationship, where I have the opportunity to pour out all my thoughts, accomplishments, and failures without concern of being misunderstood. I can place all my worries and petitions in his hands, and because I have asked, he will answer me. He will provide me with direction, and although I may not always listen or respond as I should, I know he is always there for me. I have but to ask, and he is full of forgiveness for my wrongdoings.

So as I meditate, thinking of this awesome God of mine, I wonder if I can live up to the title of "own Grandma" and all the trust and faith that these small children have placed in me. It now seems to me that my special name comes accompanied by an awesome responsibility! I pray that God will help me live up to it and that

I will be able to imitate him by always being there to love, listen, and freely forgive any transgressions. I hope that I will be able to fulfill this role now and in the future, for all the grandchildren God may choose to send. No matter how many I am blessed with, may I always be each grandchild's "own Grandma."

Love Is Like a River
By Mark Jameson*

Jesus said to him, "One who has bathed does not need to wash, except for the feet, but is entirely clean. And you are clean, though not all of you." (John 13:10)

On New Year's Day about ten years ago, I set myself a personal goal: to know deeper intimacy with Jesus during the coming year. More than ever in my life—and probably especially because I was in pain from the collapse of some close relationships—I thirsted to know his love. "Why did things fall apart the way they did?" I would ask myself. "What did I do wrong?"

I tried to sort through the pain of these broken relationships as I had always worked through difficulties: by pushing myself to get closer to the Lord in the hopes that he would heal me. I frequented the sacraments. I prayed every day. I read Scripture. Still, I wasn't experiencing the love of the Lord in the intimate, personal way that I so wanted. My knowledge seemed indirect—"mediated" through the words or witnesses of other people rather than flowing from a more immediate relationship.

In response, I multiplied my efforts, but still nothing broke the sadness in me or brought me any sense of consolation from God. I walked away from every prayer time feeling frustrated and anxious. "I'm not getting it," I'd tell the Lord. "What's the problem?

Maybe I should just resign myself to living with these wounds for the rest of my life."

Then, one evening in May, I finally poured out my heart to a friend who happened to be a priest. "You're working too hard," he said. "When you pray, don't try to analyze everything—and especially don't try to figure out what went wrong to cause these friends to turn on you. Prayer is a time to touch the Lord, not necessarily to work out all your problems. Instead, just breathe deeply, say the name of Jesus a few times, and relax. Picture him in your mind, or some image related to him, and let your imagination go. You may be surprised with how much the Holy Spirit can do with a quiet heart."

So the next day, when I sat down to pray, I recalled a passage from Ezekiel that pictured God's love like a small stream that becomes a river powerful enough to bear you up and draw you into his presence (Ezekiel 47:1-12). "Okay," I said. "I'll just imagine a little brook." Then, trying my best to relax, I took a few deep breaths and asked Jesus to be with me.

In my mind, I pictured cool, clear water bubbling up around my feet and tried to imagine how refreshing that water would feel. Then the most amazing thing happened. The image of my feet standing in a little brook shifted to an image of Jesus kneeling before me, pouring water over my feet instead. I could see that my feet were bloodied and bruised, and that bits of glass and jagged thorns were lodged in them. And there was Jesus, bent over my feet with a look of great compassion and concern. He gently began to pick out all the junk and wash the blood away. He even kissed my feet.

Then, his words pierced me to the heart. "You are already clean. Yes, you have suffered a painful loss, but it didn't happen because I am punishing you. It didn't happen because you're no good. All you need is for me to pick out the little shards and splinters that you've picked up. These shards and splinters are the inevitable result of trying to follow me in a fallen world."

I felt such love at that moment, and such a conviction that everything was going to be all right. I just needed to let Jesus minister to me, and that was a whole new revelation. For years I had been a hard worker, especially when it came to the spiritual life. *I* was going to be the one to achieve holiness. *I* was the one who would make myself useful and pleasing to the Lord. But now that I had come to the end of my rope, I discovered that all my striving and hard work were as nothing compared to the love and grace Jesus wanted to pour over me. Even if I never put in another marathon of prayer and Scripture reading, even if I never made one more sacrifice of self-denial, Jesus would still love me. He would still call me his beloved son.

I wouldn't exactly call this a mystical vision. It was more an image in my mind and an impression on my heart. There was no real water, and there were no audible words. But the sense of peace and calm was definitely real.

That one prayer time revolutionized the way I thought about God and about myself. It helped me to accept that I had failings and wounds and weaknesses, but that none of them kept God from loving me and wanting to bless me. Without giving up the fight against sin, I stopped striving to earn his love.

My prayer life changed dramatically as well. I stopped worrying about whether or not I would experience God's presence or blessing in prayer. I stopped fretting over whether I was praying long enough or hard enough. Instead, my attitude became, "Here I am, Lord. What do you want to do in me today?"

I may pray a psalm, read a Scripture passage, sing a few songs, repent, or reflect—whatever I feel inclined to do. And even if I don't "feel" Jesus' blessing, I still know that he is with me, pouring out love. How do I know this? Because when I was at my most needy and at my least able to earn his grace, he washed my feet and told me I was clean. Now I know that there's nothing like relaxing and enjoying the peace that comes from being a son of God.

A pseudonym has been used at the author's request.

5

Patience, Patience

Patience doesn't travel solo: It comes accompanied by an entourage of qualities that make for peaceful, joyful living. Just try writing a job description for patience, and you'll see how many other virtues are gathered under its umbrella.

Patience has to do with bearing pains and trials calmly, being steadfast, and putting aside hastiness and impetuosity. In our relationships with others, it involves forbearance—treating others gently and charitably and not giving in to impatience or irritability. Christian patience is grounded in the virtue of hope, which confidently looks forward to the Lord's return in glory.

Patience is one of those quiet, humble virtues that sits in the background, not looking very spectacular. But don't be fooled by appearances! It's patient endurance that wins the race. As the Letter to the Hebrews says, it is through faith and patience that we will "inherit the promises" and enter into the kingdom of heaven (Hebrews 6:12).

Think About It!

Here are two observations on patience from that master spiritual director and teacher of prayer, St. Francis de Sales: "Know that patience is the one virtue which gives greatest assurance of our reaching perfection (James 1:4) and, while we must have patience with others, we must also have it with ourselves."

Pray It!

Focus your prayer on whichever of these Scripture texts especially speaks to your heart today.

Those who wait for the LORD shall renew their strength, they shall mount up with wings like eagles, they shall run and not be weary, they shall walk and not faint. (Isaiah 40:31)

My brothers and sisters, whenever you face trials of any kind, consider it nothing but joy, because you know that the testing of your faith produces endurance; and let endurance have its full effect, so that you may be mature and complete, lacking in nothing. (James 1:2-4)

Be patient, therefore, beloved, until the coming of the Lord. The farmer waits for the precious crop from the earth, being patient with it until it receives the early and the late rains. You also must be patient. Strengthen your hearts, for the coming of the Lord is near. (James 5:7-8)

The Sarah in Me
By Barbara A. Ramian
Northbridge, Massachusetts

The LORD did for Sarah as he had promised. Sarah conceived and bore Abraham a son in his old age. (Genesis 21:1-2)

Anyone who is familiar with the Old Testament knows the story of Abraham, Sarah, and Isaac, the long-awaited son whom the Lord promised to them. Somewhat less familiar is the story of Abraham's other son, Ishmael. It is this lesser known part of the story that caught my attention several years ago.

Abram was old, and Sarai, who had never been able to conceive, was past her childbearing years when the Lord promised Abram descendants as numerous as the stars of the skies: "Your own son shall be your heir" (Genesis 15:4). After some time had passed without the Lord making good on his promise, Sarai apparently decided to take matters into her own hands. She told Abram to have sexual relations with her Egyptian maid, Hagar. "Behold now, the LORD has prevented me from bearing children; go in to my maid; it may be that I shall obtain children by her" (16:2). Hagar did indeed conceive and bear a son, whom the Lord instructed her to name Ishmael. But Sarai's plan backfired. Not only did she still not have a son of her own, she was also treated with contempt by Hagar.

When Abram was ninety-nine years old, the Lord made a covenant with him and changed his name to Abraham, signifying that he would be the father of many nations. Sarai's name was changed to Sarah (Genesis 17). In the course of time, Sarah saw God's words fulfilled: she gave birth to Isaac, the son whom the Lord had promised (21:2).

Like Sarai, we are often tempted to take matters into our own hands instead of waiting for the good that the Lord has promised us. I know how easy it is to give in to this temptation, because I too am guilty.

A few years ago, feeling tired and frustrated in my job as a parish religious education director, I decided to look for a new job. I didn't want to just continue the same work in a new parish—I wanted a real change. I updated my resume and sent it to the Catholic high schools in the area, but even as I did, I felt unsure. I really didn't want to teach high school. "But what else can I do with a degree in religious education?" I asked myself.

Almost immediately, I was contacted by one of the schools and asked to come in for an interview. It went well, but I left feeling somewhat ambivalent, without any real excitement at the prospect of being offered the job. Two days later, I was offered the position—and at a higher salary than I had expected. Still uncertain, I accepted it. I would be teaching an introductory Old Testament course to freshmen and an overview of the New Testament to sophomores.

The first few days of school started out well enough, but the job just didn't feel right. By the end of September, I knew I had made the wrong choice. On the surface, all appeared well. The teachers and administrators were kind and welcoming. My students, for the most part, were wonderful. I made more money than I had made before. I worked Monday through Friday with weekends off, a luxury I never had in my parish job. Plus, there were the school vacations.

But I wasn't happy. As I drove up the long driveway in front of the school each morning at seven o'clock, I couldn't wait for three o'clock to arrive. On Monday I was already looking forward to Friday. I started to cross the days off on my calendar, something I hadn't done since I was a little girl counting the days until Christmas. Despite everyone's attempts to make me feel at home, I felt like a guest in someone else's home. I longed for the familiarity of my parish job and thought of dozens of things I would do differently, if only I could return.

In the late fall, my freshman classes studied the story of Abraham and Sarah. As we went through the story together, the truth of my own impatience and lack of trust in God became painfully obvious to me. Like Sarai, I had not wanted to wait for the Lord but had taken matters into my own hands. Instead of turning to God for guidance when feeling down about my parish job, I had quit and had taken a job that was never meant for me. Like Sarai's plan, mine had backfired.

With God's help, I made it through the school year. When it ended, I returned to my parish job with a new attitude and a renewed sense of purpose. Instead of imagining that I would be better off somewhere else, I gave myself wholeheartedly to my work. In the process, many doors were opened to me. I have been led into new areas of ministry right here within my parish.

Looking back on that year, I have no regrets. In fact, I am grateful. It was a valuable learning experience. I made the acquaintance of some wonderful people, two of whom have become very dear friends. I learned many lessons as I journeyed through the Scriptures with my students. Most of all, I learned to trust in the Lord and listen for his guidance instead of becoming impatient and taking matters into my own hands.

I admit that even now, I sometimes find myself starting to panic because my life isn't going exactly as I want it to. In those moments, I am still tempted to take control and try to fix things, to move them along a little. But always, by the grace of God, I remember the story of Sarai, and I manage to stop myself in time.

In his infinite wisdom, God allowed me to take control for a while—just long enough to learn that I can't rely only on my own power and insight. And so each day that I come to work, I give thanks for the opportunity to serve the Lord right where I am. I look forward to the next stage of my journey, knowing that when the time is right to move on, the Lord will let me know.

What I Learned Pulling Teeth
By James Birong
Carrollton, Ohio

God opposes the proud,
but gives grace to the humble. (James 4:6)

It didn't look to be a difficult job. As a dentist who had been in practice for a good number of years, I had extracted many teeth. Besides, this patient was an older gentleman whose four wisdom teeth were not beneath the gum. "Should be easy to get them out," I thought to myself. I usually say a prayer before beginning to work on a patient, but I was feeling so confident that I probably neglected to do so.

I soon discovered that the job wasn't going to be so simple. After an hour and ten minutes, which is the amount of time I had scheduled for this patient, I was just on the third tooth. When I finally managed to get it out, I was twenty minutes behind. By then, I had prayed several times, asking that the procedure go smoothly. Feeling anxious and pressured, I started on the last tooth. I pushed and pulled, but it would not move. I got a heavier instrument and pushed a little harder. SNAP! The crown broke off—but still, no movement of the tooth itself.

I found myself getting somewhat upset. "Lord, please help me to get this out *now*!" I pushed and pushed. No progress. I was getting angry. The next patient had already been kept waiting an hour, and the following patient had just arrived. "Lord, do you want me to hurt this man and keep these people waiting? I *need* your help!" I continued pushing for another ten minutes. Another piece of the tooth broke off, and still no movement. Realizing that I was getting nowhere, I stopped to reflect.

For whatever reason, God was not stepping in to make this easy. But wasn't it foolish of me to get mad at God for not helping? How did I know what his plan was? Various possibilities crossed my mind. *Maybe this is supposed to be training in patience for me and for this man.... Maybe the people in the waiting room have found a good religious magazine and are really growing in faith....* I decided to quit worrying. No sense my trying to rush—that tooth would come out only in God's good time. Meanwhile, I recognized that I needed to repent. "Lord, I'm sorry for my anxiety and my anger," I prayed. "Forgive me for trying to give you orders. I'll do my best with this extraction, but now I'm leaving the timing in your hands." Then I felt a real peace. I had turned the job over to God. The pressure was off. If the secretary had to reschedule appointments for people in the waiting room, so be it.

I picked up my instrument to start again. I pushed a little and saw a little movement. I pushed a second time, and the root popped right out. Wow! My attitude had been the problem! How could the Lord help someone who was angry, impatient, and failing to trust him? What a fool I'd been. I had prayed while still trying to do it all myself. When I let go and put everything in God's hands, the result was immediate.

Why does God so often seem to wait till I get desperate before answering my prayer? As I see it now, if he were to answer sooner, my pride would step in. I might think I'd figured out how to manipulate him or resolve a problem without his help. But when I come to the Lord with humble awareness of both my need and his sovereignty, then I can recognize and thank him when he answers, instead of jumping to the wrong conclusions. Truly, "God opposes the proud, but gives grace to the humble" (James 4:6)!

The Lord, My Protector
By Herbert Rodriguez
Miami, Florida

I look to the mountains; where will my help come from?
My help will come from the LORD, who made heaven and earth.
(Psalm 121:1-2, Today's English Version)

"Through fire comes purification," people say. But not until the heat comes into our own kitchen do we really understand this process and what it involves. How we handle that "heat" when it does come can either make us stronger than ever before, or it can destroy our spirit and affect our friends and loved ones as well.

One summer about five years ago, the flames came my way. I didn't see them coming. After years of "doing the right thing" and climbing the corporate ladder, I had successfully established profitable international operations for multinational corporations. My wife's career was also moving along. We had just been blessed by the birth of a beautiful, healthy baby girl.

Within forty-five days of her birth, in the dawn of my new family life, my world came tumbling down, or so I thought. I lost my job and was mystified and shocked to find myself caught in an unbelievable and unjust corporate situation. The stress of this fiasco compounded the effects of other serious challenges I had experienced within the previous two years. I had lost my twin brother to a terminal illness. My best friend had just had coronary bypass surgery and developed complications that put him in a coma for two months. (He recovered but succumbed to other health problems in late 2001.)

At the outset of my difficulties, I found myself seeking answers to these situations that truly seemed devastating. Having been raised a Catholic, with a solid foundation in our faith, I was challenged to understand and find meaning in what I was confronting. I must admit that my initial focus centered on the question, "How could God permit this injustice to happen to me?" I soon discovered that there were no "human" answers. And the more I tried to engineer and control the outcome of my situation, the farther away any satisfying resolution seemed to be.

It is true that the Spirit works in mysterious ways. Because I felt so helpless, I found myself trying to listen more attentively for the Spirit's guidance. I turned to reading Scripture, meditating, and putting the outcome of my life totally in God's hands. I grew in patience. In the process, I experienced the reality of what Psalm 121 affirms about God—that he truly is my Protector and the source of all my help.

As I turned to God, many aspects of our family life began to change. We became more loving and caring of one another, more sensitive to each other's needs. We realized that Jesus' message to "love one another" is the foundation for every aspect of our lives.

Through daily spiritual meditations, Scripture reading, prayers, and working on expressing our thoughts and efforts in a positive manner, we have survived. We have even become stronger as a family. We have realized what is of real value in life. God has increased our sense of hope, peace, and love and is teaching us how to live and raise our daughter in accordance with his will.

In God's good time, other things also worked out. Today, I work with a major corporation and am facing my biggest career challenges ever. I am happy to tackle them, and I am doing fine. Although it did not seem so five years ago, I have no doubt that what happened to me then was the biggest blessing in disguise I could ever have hoped for. In both my personal and professional life, I am reaping the benefits of what I learned about patience and priorities.

My mother, who is the original rock of faith in our family, has always reminded us to trust in the Lord and listen for his guidance. This was difficult at first, but her patience, persistence, and love have been a confirming example that "the Lord is our Protector." I refer to Psalm 121 whenever I need reminding. During trying or tranquil times, it gives me strength to keep moving patiently forward, with my Protector leading the way.

I look to the mountains; where will my help come from? My help will come from the LORD, who made heaven and earth.

He will not let you fall; your protector is always awake. The protector of Israel never dozes or sleeps.

The LORD will guard you; he is by your side to protect you. The sun will not hurt you during the day, nor the moon by night.

The LORD will protect you from all danger; he will keep you safe. He will protect you as you come and go now and forever.

Journey of Joy
By Caroline Cella
Massapequa, New York

My brothers and sisters, whenever you face trials of any kind, consider it nothing but joy. (James 1:2)

A cradle Catholic and the product of Catholic grammar and high schools, I never read an entire book of the Bible until I took a course to be certified as a teacher for a sixth-grade religious education class. For homework, Sister instructed us to prayerfully read just one portion of God's "love letter" to us, the Letter of James. My attraction to God's word was immediate. Even as I read with wonder (how could one be joyful in trials?), I was encouraged to discover more.

Chapter three of James speaks about the need to control the tongue. Since I didn't have a very good tongue at that time, I was persuaded that improvement was needed. And so began the journey of joy and love—of reading God's word and receiving guidance and hope—that has sustained me for the past thirty years.

The more I studied, the more I wanted to know. I subscribed to several Scripture magazines whose daily readings supplied me with some knowledge and answers I could apply to my life experiences. Reflecting on Scripture, I was led to deeper prayer and surrender. I attended a prayer group and met with friends to discuss God's word. Along the way, I discovered many special verses that strengthened and encouraged me. Ultimately, all of this awakened a desire to teach, which in turn led me to an undergraduate and then a masters degree in theology.

I had wanted to be a teacher since I was fifteen years old, but I was almost forty—married with two children—when I began working on a college degree part time. Despite the competing pulls of school and family responsibilities, I was able to persevere and "count it all joy" amid the trials because I sensed that God was leading me to wonderful new places. God's word held me together, even providing insight into how to interpret my various experiences.

Much to my surprise, God had not forgotten that prayer from my teenage years. At forty-five, I was hired to teach religion in a Catholic high school. After delighting in this position for six years, I was laid off due to financial cutbacks. In that time of great uncertainty, Jeremiah 29:11 invited me to trust: "For surely I know the plans I have for you, says the LORD, plans for your welfare and not for harm, to give you a future with hope." These encouraging words nourished me, though I walked in mystery for quite a while, doubtful and questioning.

With no teaching position in sight, I took a job as a parish director of religious education. Though not my first choice, the job proved a blessing. It enabled me to spend more time with my mother, who was elderly and ill. With the grace of God, those two years saw the healing of many hurts in our relationship.

Still, I missed the classroom and invariably found myself drawn to readings from the "exile" period of the Hebrew Scriptures. God gave me many verses about restoration. I read and wondered about them for a long time, always struggling to "consider it nothing but joy." Finally, I was indeed "restored." The school where I had taught asked me to return. Now my life mirrored an exile and a restoration. The experience had changed me, I realized. Through the difficulties, I had been healed and made whole in a way that would not have been possible in more peaceful circumstances. Luke 5:38—"new wine must be put into fresh wineskins"—took on a personal meaning.

Two years later, the pastor invited me to join the parish staff as director of religious formation for adults. Because of my experience in the "exile" period of my life, I sensed a further calling and accepted. I am now able to teach the Bible to interested, hungry adults on the parish level—planting seeds that God will water, I am sure. If I had never lost my teaching job, would I be here today? God took what I considered one of the worst events of my life and worked it for good, as Romans 8:28 declares.

While I have some biblical knowledge now, I intend to keep learning. God's mercies are new each day, offering an inexhaustible source of love, guidance, and nourishment to drink in and share with others. During Lent, I was led to read Romans 12 each day. It was a remarkable renewal. Along with James 1:2, Romans 12:12 has become my mainstay: "Rejoice in hope, be patient in suffering, persevere in prayer." The journey continues, and I am so grateful that God's "love letter" remains active and alive.

Patience Begins at Home
By Michael Rosslund*

My child, help your father in his old age, and do not grieve him as long as he lives; even if his mind fails, be patient with him; because you have all your faculties do not despise him. For kindness to a father will not be forgotten, and will be credited to you against your sins. (Sirach 3:12-14)

It was the first Sunday after Christmas, the Feast of the Holy Family, and the reading from Sirach really struck me. A doctor had just confirmed our suspicions that my father's forgetfulness, repetitiveness, and uncharacteristic paranoia were beyond the normal range for someone his age. Yes, Dad had Alzheimer's.

"Even if his mind fails, be patient with him" (Sirach 3:13). I knew it wouldn't be easy to follow Sirach's exhortation. But along with grief and fear, I felt a deep sense of gratitude as I listened to that reading. God had been preparing me for the challenge, I realized. Some years before, when my father's mind was still healthy and active, God had directed my attention to the impatient manner with which I treated my closest relatives, especially my father. He had helped me to recognize and fight this tendency by leading me into what I suspect will be lifelong training in humility, kindness, and respect for others.

Perhaps my lack of patience with Dad was especially pronounced because we were so similar. Each of us was quick to grasp problems and propose solutions; we were each thorough, creative, forceful—and, it must be said, rather stubborn about doing things our own way. Early on, I felt the clash as Dad "helped" me with science projects, math assignments, and building a tree house. "Let me do it," I'd beg him. But as I experienced it, my father took over every time. Frustrated, I gradually distanced myself and stopped looking to him for practical help and instruction.

Eventually, though, I began suspecting that my attitude was a major part of the problem. It hit me that my siblings were learning a lot from watching and doing things with Dad, and that they seemed to enjoy the process. Some were acquiring his skill at gourmet cooking; others were becoming accomplished at carpentry or chess. Seeing this, I began to wonder: Maybe there was something prideful and distorted about my extreme desire to learn and do things "by myself." Maybe I was impatient—too impatient to learn from my father and simply enjoy being with him.

Fortunately, I came to this realization while Dad and I still had opportunities to spend time together. One day, somewhat tentatively, I asked him for advice about repairing a canoe. That experience was far more helpful and enjoyable than I had expected. It opened a door and marked a turning point in our relationship.

Despite my good intentions, I didn't always find it easy to curb my impatience with Dad. But as I struggled, Scripture and the Holy Spirit came to my help. Various Bible verses took on new meaning and inspired me to persevere. I reflected often on "children's duties toward parents" in Sirach 3:1-16. I became more motivated to pursue patience once I noticed how important it is. Patience is the first characteristic highlighted in St. Paul's classic description of love (1 Corinthians 13:4); it's listed among the fruits of the Spirit (Galatians 5:22). How could I have overlooked it for so long?

By the time my father's health began declining, he and I had developed a close relationship marked by mutual respect and lively give-and-take. Now, I'm counting on this firm foundation and on God's grace to see us through this last and difficult phase of Dad's life. Aware of my weakness but certain of God's faithfulness and mercy, I will keep pursuing the goal to which St. Paul calls us all: "to lead a life worthy of the calling to which you have been called, with all humility and gentleness, with patience, bearing with one another in love" (Ephesians 4:1-2).

A pseudonym has been used at the author's request.

6

Guide My Steps

You're at your wits' end. You have a decision to make or a problem to solve. Or maybe someone is looking to you for advice that you don't really have. So you do the only logical thing: You pray, "Help, Lord! I need wisdom!" And whether right away or over time, whether through a person, a book, an event, a thought, or something else entirely, the Holy Spirit nudges you in the right direction. For the people who contributed the stories in this chapter, guidance came through the Spirit-inspired words of Scripture.

Maybe you have experienced for yourself that the Bible is an inspired and inspiring word. Just as God inspired those who wrote and edited it, he wishes to inspire us as we read it. If we approach Scripture with faith and expectation, God will reveal himself to us, shedding light on our paths and problems.

When we read the Bible, how can we know whether we are being guided by God and not just by our own ideas? While there is no formulaic approach to this question, the answer has to do with reading the Bible not as a lone individual, but as a member of one body, the Church.

As members of that body, we are blessed with the teaching office of the pope and bishops, who are guided by the Spirit to interpret Scripture in an authentic and authoritative way. We can allow ourselves to be trained and formed by the teachers the Church commissions, who preach and interpret God's word. As we look for guidance through Scripture, we need to approach our own insights and inspirations with care and discernment, always seeking the help of that same Holy Spirit who guides the Church as a whole. We may want to seek out a pastor, spiritual director, or trusted friend to help us in that discernment process.

Think About It!

St. Vincent de Paul's advice about prayer applies to Scripture reading as well:

> When any question arises, turn to God and say to him, "Lord, you who are the source of knowledge, show me what I ought to do...." Ask yourself: "Does this agree with our Lord's teaching?" If you feel it does, hurry to do it; if not, you must decide against it.

Pray It!

"Your word is a lamp to my feet and a light to my path" (Psalm 119:105). May I never open your word without praying, "Come, Holy Spirit! Please speak to me." May I always listen actively and attentively, ready to hear and obey.

Prescription from the Great Physician
By Isagani L. Landicho
Quezon City, Philippines

*Honor physicians for their services, for the Lord created them;
for their gift of healing comes from the Most High.
(Sirach 38:1-2)*

One rainy November, I led a survey team into the hill country about seventy-five miles northwest of Manila. Because of the intermittent bad weather that blanketed us at the site, the project was unduly prolonged. After three weeks, I returned home exhausted. Three days later, as I was walking to work, I suddenly felt a squeezing chest pain that forced me to buckle down to the pavement. I didn't panic but slowly took deep breaths and prayed for a few minutes. God came quickly to my aid, and I was guided home.

The experience was an eye-opener. I was fifty-one years old, with a wonderful wife and three children in school. I had never been confronted with any sign of heart trouble, but I guessed that the stress of the past three weeks had triggered my near collapse. A series of tests confirmed that I had serious heart disease and needed immediate bypass surgery. Since the cost was beyond what an ordinary income earner like myself could afford, however, I decided to just continue on my medication indefinitely.

My condition was like a buried seed that slowly pushes up as a sprout above the earth. Troubling signs began to emerge, causing me tremendous worries. Walking became an effort. Climbing stairs was too strenuous. I followed my doctor's advice—routine exercise, a low-salt and low-fat diet, medication, and stress management. But the most helpful remedy came as I learned to turn to God in a deeper way.

At that time, my wife began attending a charismatic prayer meeting. I was unfamiliar with this style of prayer, but I welcomed the bright outlook of getting closer to God and started to accompany her. As my physical condition worsened, I turned in faith to the Lord and asked for healing. Group members prayed over me often. Whenever they did, dark clouds of anxiety gave way to the calm, bright light of peace. Eventually, though, the signs of my illness would always recur.

One evening while I was walking home from a prayer meeting, a sudden shooting pain seized me again. Immediately, I reached into my pocket for the emergency tablet I always carried with me. I put it under my tongue and rested on the roadside, crying to the Lord for help. It came to me that when I got home, I should pray as Matthew 6:6 advises: "Go into your room and shut the door and pray to your Father." I did exactly that. Entering my room, I closed the door and knelt before the three-foot crucifix on the wall. "Lord," I prayed, "I know how much you love me. How could I have survived all these difficult days if you had not been keeping me alive?" Then I asked, "Father, what shall I do?"

As I waited in silence, I had a mental impression of a distinct figure saying, "Read Sirach 38." The words were clear, but they struck me as strange. I was unfamiliar with the word "Sirach." It slowly dawned on me that Sirach was probably a book of the Bible, and 38, a chapter number.

Immediately, I gave thanks and praise. Filled with expectation, I turned on the light, found our Bible lying on the shelf, and dusted it off. My excitement mounted as I scanned the table of contents and discovered the book of Sirach. My heart beating faster, I flipped the pages quickly to chapter 38. And behold, the first verse said it all: "Honor physicians for their services, for the Lord created them; for their gift of healing comes from the Most

High"! What a bull's-eye! All I had wanted was to evade surgery, but here was my God pointing to a possibility I had not wanted to consider. Then and there, I changed course. "Father, if this is what you want, I'll follow you without reservation, regardless of cost."

About a week later, I underwent a quintuple heart bypass operation. Three weeks later, I was back to work! The finances worked out, too. Thanks to my doctors, my hospital bill was reduced by 25 percent; my employee medical coverage was almost sufficient for the remaining expenses.

Imagine my amazement when I discovered that I was able to climb all the way to the top of our nineteen-story office building! I was so excited that I gave myself high-fives, right there at the top of the stairs!

Today, twenty years and another bypass operation later, I'm seventy-three and still in very good health. Thank you, Father, for restoring me to health and for letting me know your love through the skills of dedicated physicians, sharers in your gift of healing.

The Key Ring and the Kingdom
By Jean Hampton
Old Lyme, Connecticut

With God all things are possible. (Matthew 19:26)

My beloved dad was in his late eighties and enjoyed good health until he developed a severe heart problem. He was a spiritual person, although this had not been true when he was a younger man. But for years now, he had been reading his Bible every day.

We often discussed Scripture, and one day my father came to me quite agitated. He had just read the story about Jesus' encounter with the rich young man, which ends: "Jesus said to him, 'If you would be perfect, go, sell what you possess and give to the poor, and you will have treasure in heaven; and come, follow me.' When the young man heard this he went away sorrowful; for he had great possessions" (Matthew 19:21-22).

Dad had an intuition that he did not have much time left on this earth, and after reading this Scripture passage, he was sure that he was not eligible for heaven. He was not a millionaire, but he did have a considerable amount of money saved and a store of valuable possessions garnered over the years. I tried to encourage Dad, because he had been so generous, faithful, and true, yet he "went away sorrowful" and troubled about what he owned. "I know I am not worthy of heaven," he said to me at the close of our conversation.

Not many months later, my father died quite suddenly of a heart attack. My own heart ached as I remembered his worry about not going to heaven. Another year or so passed, and still I wondered about the answer to this all-important question. Was Dad in heaven or not? Deep in my heart, I believed that such a good man would not be denied entrance, yet the question still nagged at me.

For many years I had carried a key ring that my father gave me when I was quite young. I had gotten so used to it that I never paid it any attention. Then one day, out of nowhere, a light seemed to shine on the key ring, and I took a close look at what was written on it. To my amazement and delight, what I read there were the very words Jesus spoke to the disciples when they asked him, "Who then can be saved?"

"With men this is impossible, but with God all things are possible" (Matthew 19:26).

I had received the assurance I needed!

Are You Ready?
By Ngozi Mosindi
Lagos, Nigeria

My sheep hear my voice. I know them, and they follow me.
I give them eternal life, and they will never perish.
(John 10:27-28)

I began hearing the voice of the Good Shepherd when I picked up an old copy of *The Word Among Us* at a friend's home two years ago. It was an Advent issue. The cover caption—"Are You Ready?"—caught my attention, and I asked to borrow the magazine. I took my time studying it and found that the readings touched me and also led me to ask myself a whole lot of questions. "What is it that is keeping me far from God?... What am I doing that I'm not supposed to do?" This prompted me to become more serious about developing and strengthening my relationship with God.

Several weeks later, I boarded a twelve-passenger taxi going to another city. We were moving along quite normally when suddenly our vehicle collided head-on with a bus. Everything went blank. Then I heard shouts and tried to open my eyes, but something was blocking my vision. I couldn't raise my left hand, and when I managed to wipe my face with my right hand, I realized that it was covered with blood.

I heard a loud banging noise, and rescuers started tearing the taxi apart to get us out. Looking around, I could see very faintly that it was crushed and that bodies were scattered everywhere. I started praying, "God, help me to live. But if I die, receive my soul and have mercy on me." I said the *Our Father* and *Hail Mary*, and then I cried for help. Finally some other survivors and I were put into a car and driven to the hospital.

As we lay there on the ground outside the hospital, waiting for nurses to attend to us, rescuers brought in more people from the accident scene. Some were dying; others were already dead. Wailing and crying filled the air. All this while, I kept praying and asking God to help me endure. One prayer was answered when a hospital official noticed that I was conscious and took down my name and emergency contact information. Thanks to a series of providential circumstances, he was able to notify my family and my office colleagues. They arrived just in time to take me by ambulance to a larger hospital where I would receive better treatment.

Eventually, I discovered the extent of my injuries—multiple fractures in my left arm and leg, a fractured pelvis, multiple cuts and lacerations. I also learned how fortunate I had been: Along with one little boy whose mother died in the crash, I was the only other survivor. "Why am I alive?" I asked myself. "I'm no more deserving than the sixteen people who died." Then, realizing that I would never be able to penetrate this mystery, I simply thanked God for his tender mercies and prayed that he would show me how to respond.

I spent about four months in the hospital. The experience gave me a chance to observe and reflect on many things. I saw that the hospital beds were never empty. People came in with cancer, AIDS, and a host of other ailments and injuries. Many died. Some who lived went home after undergoing amputations.

I came face to face with the fragility of life. It struck me that none of us knows what's going to happen even in the next minute. I concluded that the best option is to surrender one-self to the One who knows all. Even more firmly, I resolved to "get ready" and to follow the Good Shepherd even more closely. Having already experienced his protection, I knew that no matter what happened to me, all would be well with him by my side. This promise saw me through every trauma.

While in the hospital, I started reading the Bible and pray-ing the rosary regularly. A priest came in often to give me Communion. And thank God for my roommates! Together we read the word of God and listened to gospel music, which lifted our spirits.

When I left the hospital in May, I went to my parish priest and poured out my heart in confession—something I hadn't done in three years. Afterward I felt so happy and free. I told my friends about God's goodness, and they saw it demonstrated in my rapid recovery, which was something of a miracle. No limping, no nagging pains, no HIV (which had been a real pos-sibility, considering the massive blood transfusions I received).

What a sweet relief!

I know my Good Shepherd better now, and I turn to my Bible often as I continue to seek his guidance. I still pray that I will follow as he leads me where he wants me to go. Most of all, I count on his promise of protection to all his sheep: "I give them eternal life, and they will never perish" (John 10:28).

How Will I Know God's Voice?
By Ann Hegelheimer
St. Thomas, Ontario, Canada

I am the vine, you are the branches. (John 15:5)

After ten years of not practicing my Catholic faith, the Holy Spirit really touched my life and I returned to the Church. I started asking my friends questions like "How can you know when God is speaking to you? Do you actually hear a voice?" Their reply was always: "You'll know." "How will I know?" I'd persist. Then they'd answer, "You'll just know, that's all."

During the time when I was wondering how to hear God, a friend gave me a Christian tape. I listened to it, but afterward all I remembered was the line, "I am the vine, you are the branches." The following Sunday at Mass, there it was again, in the gospel reading: "I am the vine, you are the branches. Those who abide in me and I in them bear much fruit, because apart from me you can do nothing" (John 15:5). "Strange," I thought. "What a coincidence." For just a little while, it made me think.

Several months later, my husband and I traveled to another city to attend a Catholic conference. Instead of booking a hotel room there as we normally did, we stayed at the home of our best friends, who had offered us the use of their house while they were on a trip to France.

At first, I found the conference uninteresting. I began to wonder why I was there, as I didn't feel I was getting anything out of it. But my attitude did a sudden about-face when one of the speakers began talking about … yes, the vine and the branches! He explored the subject in great depth, and I knew then that God had wanted me at that conference for a reason. By this time, I was no longer wondering whether I would ever be able to hear and know God's voice. I was certain that God was the one speaking to me through John 15:5.

Before God drew my attention to this Scripture passage, I tended to approach my spiritual life in a rather self-reliant way, as if my relationship with God depended mostly on my own initiative and effort. That began to change as I meditated on the image of the vine and the branches. I saw that although I was just a tiny branch, I would receive God's very own abundant life and power if only I stayed connected to Jesus, the vine. Without God, I am nothing and cannot live. But with God's life and energy sustaining me, I can grow and produce a hundredfold! What a revelation this was for me!

After our friends returned from France, we drove back to visit with them. They gave us a bottle of holy water from Lourdes, then handed me another gift. What I saw when I opened the box surprised me so much that I dropped it on the coffee table and exclaimed, "I can't believe this!" My friends watched with amazement, wondering why I had gotten so excited over a box of chocolates. When I explained about John 15:5, though, they understood immediately. For those were no ordinary chocolates in that gift box—they were chocolates in the shape of grapevines!

Praise God, who finds so many ways of speaking to us!

My Three Horses
By Davin Winger
Gruver, Texas

If anyone serves me, he must follow me, and where I am, there shall my servant be also. (John 12:26)

We have three horses on the Winger place. Their names are Smokey, Turtle, and Spuds, and they each have their own personality. Smokey is the oldest. Turtle is the best athlete and the fastest. Spuds is the biggest and also the slowest.

Have you ever led a horse? You know the old saying, "You can lead a horse to water, but you can't make him drink." I have seen that happen many times. Sometimes you know that horse has to be thirsty, but he just won't drink.

Leading each one of our horses is an entirely different experience. When I try to lead Smokey through the gate, he balks. I have to pull and pull at his reins and sometimes turn him around and start over. When I start to lead Turtle, he wants to walk right beside me. Sometimes he even gets ahead of me, and he doesn't even know where I'm going. I think he just likes being the boss. Spuds, however, is a pleasure to lead. As I start to walk off, he gets right behind me and follows. I don't have to pull on the reins—in fact, they are loose in my hands. When I stop, Spuds stops, and usually he doesn't even step on my feet!

As I've observed my three horses, they've taught me something about how I relate to God. I've had to ask myself: Which "horse" am I? Do I balk when God tries to lead me somewhere, like Smokey does? Am I like Turtle, wanting God to do things my way and always getting ahead of him without even knowing where he is going?

I want to be like Spuds—quietly following my master, walking when he walks, stopping when he stops, turning when he turns.

Being There
By Rita M. Keylor
Auburn, Maine

And remember, I am with you always, to the end of the age.
(Matthew 28:20)

My husband was very ill. I had done everything I could to find something that would help him, but I could see that he was not getting better. Despite the wonderful nurses and aides from hospice, the doctors' appointments, medications, and everything else, he was getting weaker. It bothered me terribly to see him in such declining health.

One night, I was thinking about how Jesus promised to be with us always. I told God that I believed this with my whole heart. Then I asked him to show me whether there was anything else I could do to help my husband.

I received my answer the very next morning. It was a "first Friday," and I went to Mass. I had just gone into the church and was kneeling to say my prayers. I wasn't thinking at all about my prayer of the previous evening, when I heard an inner voice say very clearly, "Just be there." I felt so relieved and reassured! God had shown me that he keeps his promises, and also that I was not leaving anything undone in helping my husband.

My husband died a few months later, and I knew that it was time for him to go home to God. As I remember how God encouraged me to keep on being there for my husband, I rejoice knowing that God will always "be there" for me.

Crying to the Lord
By Heather Stevinson
Mt. Sterling, Illinois

---

*He did not hide his face from me, but heard when
I cried to him. (Psalm 22:24)*

It was the middle of October. Three weeks previously, I had given birth to our son, Joseph.

Before Joseph was born, I led an active prayer life. In the early morning, I would spend time praying the rosary or in meditation and supplication to Jesus. After we brought Joseph home, though, I barely had time to take a shower, let alone sit in prayer for almost an hour. It hardly seemed possible to seek God's presence and guidance any longer. As the days passed, I stopped trying.

As parents know, newborn babies cry—sometimes a lot! That October day was one of those times, and I was distraught. I had tried everything and didn't know what else to do. Should I let Joseph "cry it out" or keep trying to calm him?

With my son wailing in the background—and myself crying as well—I dropped to my knees, looked at the crucifix on the wall, and asked God to help me find guidance in my Bible. I closed my eyes and opened my Bible, trusting that God would find a way to bless me with wisdom for my situation. When I looked down, I found myself reading Psalm 22, which begins with the words Jesus prayed from the cross: "My God, my God, why have you forsaken me? Why are you so far from helping me, from the words of my groaning?" (verse 1). Reading on, I felt the Holy Spirit's presence:

> Yet it was you who took me from the womb;
> you kept me safe on my mother's breast.
> On you I was cast from my birth,
> and since my mother bore me you have been my God.
> Do not be far from me,
> for trouble is near and there is no one to help....
> He did not hide his face from me,
> but heard when I cried to him. (Psalm 22:9-11, 24)

My heart immediately swelled with love for my child. I went to him, knowing somehow that this was the right thing to do. In fact, never before had I felt such instant and vivid guidance, such a clear answer to my prayer! That day, in a special way, the Lord helped me to see Jesus in my tiny son.

He enlightened me in another way, too. That day, I also realized that just because I couldn't pray in one long session, it was no reason to abandon prayer altogether. I now have learned to pray each day in little bits and pieces.

My Unexpected Birthday Gift
By Fr. Carlo Notaro, D.S. Carn.
Milwaukee, Wisconsin

Go from your country and your kindred and your father's house to the land that I will show you. (Genesis 12:1)

I had planned to have a party on my eighteenth birthday. But that day at work, I hit my head on a steel beam. I was rushed to the hospital with a concussion. When I was in the hospital my hands trembled, my vision was impaired, and my walk was unsteady. I was very scared and confused. I wondered if I would ever be the same again.

In desperation, I picked up a Bible I saw on the nightstand and began reading the first chapter of Genesis. It was difficult to read, but I kept trying. When I reached Genesis 12, the story of the call of Abraham, it impressed me deeply. Perhaps I was being called to something? I thought of the possibility of a public office. It wasn't until a few years later that I realized that I had a religious calling.

Eventually I joined the Order of St. Camillus, the Servants of the Sick. St. Camillus, who is patron of the sick and nurses, was the Mother Teresa of his time. I have been blessed to be a priest working with the sick for fifteen years now. I have found that although there are many dimensions to the priesthood, the most important is celebrating the Eucharist. Other things that help me nurture my spiritual life are daily Bible reading and devotion to Mary.

I am happy. There are residual effects from the concussion, but they are minor. I still have a long ways to go in my journey, but I never stop being grateful that God called me, even as I was feeling at my weakest! My one desire for the rest of my life is to grow in Christian love as I follow Jesus day by day.

It Started with a Calendar

By Tom Krulikowski

Bethel Park, Pennsylvania

*Your word is a lamp to my feet
and a light to my path. (Psalm 119:105)*

Six years ago, as Advent was approaching, I began to feel that my relationship with God had reached a plateau. Wanting to find deeper meaning in the season, I took one of the Advent calendars provided by our parish that listed each day's liturgical readings. Then I went to a local bookstore to buy the same Bible that my two teenage daughters had used for CCD.

I brought the calendar and Bible to work with me and began to read the daily readings at lunchtime. I experienced no great conversion or powerful insight. When Advent ended, however, I wanted to keep going. I started with the gospels, with a goal to finish them by Easter. In this fashion, I read the Bible cover to cover. Then I went back to the daily readings, recognizing that, for me, this was the most fruitful way to read Scripture.

At first, my time with Scripture didn't feel very enlightening. I'd read several verses and usually didn't get a lot out of them. But gradually, I began experiencing God's word as having a miraculous impact! Practically every day, it seems, Scripture has an effect on my life.

Just in the course of an ordinary day, I'm faced with difficult issues at work, at home, or with life in general. As an engineering manager, for example, I find it easy to get so caught up in immediate problems that I either forget the people I work with or see only their shortcomings. Countless times I've been redirected by coming across a passage like 1 John 4:20-21: "For those who do not love a brother or sister whom they have seen, cannot love

God whom they have not seen. The commandment we have from him is this: those who love God must love their brothers and sisters also." In this way, the Holy Spirit routinely reminds me that all the people I see and talk to every day are children of God, people I must love.

Reading the Scriptures has helped me in my relationship with my daughters. Both are intelligent and wonderful young ladies, but as they've matured from children to teenagers, I've had to change the way I relate to them. I found this process particularly difficult with my younger daughter (whom my wife says is just like me!). For a time, I could not seem to communicate with her; in fact, all my attempts were just making things worse. Psalm 105:4 finally reminded me where to turn: "Seek the LORD and his strength; seek his presence continually." As I turned to our Lord in prayer and asked for his help, many good things happened. My daughter and I found our way through our crisis, and our father-young adult relationship is again growing.

Sometimes Scripture has spoken to me in more dramatic ways. In one period of my career, I was engaged in some heavy soul-searching about "getting ahead," struggling to find the balance between self-confidence and self-promotion. In the thick of the battle, Mark 9:35 outlined my priorities: "He sat down, called the twelve, and said to them, 'Whoever wants to be first must be last of all and servant of all.'" I know God was telling me that while he wants me to use my abilities and to work hard, my career should not come first in my life.

In my parish, I'm a cantor and choir member, and I really enjoy singing and leading the congregation in song. Perhaps it isn't surprising, then, that God has called out to me through the words of a song I particularly enjoy. One time I was inspired to volunteer more of my time after singing, "Here I am, Lord. It is I, Lord."

By reading Scripture every day, I have come to know that

Jesus is with me every moment, in everything I do. There's not one single thing I can't talk to him about! Through my time with Scripture, I am also learning how to listen more to the Holy Spirit. Already I have felt his proddings on more occasions than I can count.

Looking back, I can see now that it was the Holy Spirit who prodded me to pick up that Bible and Advent calendar six years ago. Little did I know it was the beginning of a wonderful change in my life—the discovery of a light showing me the path to greater love for Jesus.

The Perfect Word
By Kathleen Shanahan
Westerly, Rhode Island

For thus said the Lord GOD, the Holy One of Israel:
"In returning and rest you shall be saved; in quietness and
in trust shall be your strength." (Isaiah 30:15)

My mother-in-law, Rhoda, lost her husband unexpectedly on December 10, 1999. Less than a month later, her son—my husband—died of brain cancer.

A little over a year later, an MRI showed that my mother-in-law herself had (of all things) a brain tumor. Although it was benign, Rhoda was told that she needed to undergo a form of radiosurgery known as "Gamma Knife" within the month. Obviously this was a traumatic time for her. Not having her husband of almost fifty years by her side, as well as knowing that her son had died from a brain tumor, she experienced great anxiety.

I prayed to God that he would give me the right words to say to my mother-in-law to help ease her mind. I was led to pick up the Bible and started flipping through the pages. Often at a time like this, I would turn to the psalms. Instead, I found myself continuing past them and ending up in the Book of Isaiah. My eyes were drawn to Isaiah 30:15: "For thus said the Lord GOD, the Holy One of Israel: 'In returning and rest you shall be saved; in quietness and in trust shall be your strength.'"

I immediately called my mother-in-law and read her the verse, which brought her great comfort. I also decided to give her my husband's Bible with the passage highlighted. She wound up taking the Bible to the hospital when she went for the procedure. Everything went smoothly, and she is still doing fine.

How many times God has led me to read something from Scripture that was just what I needed to hear! I praise him for leading me to a passage that helped someone else.

7

A Heart for Others

A nun in Japan seeks opportunities to spread the gospel. A Florida father comes to realize that he is serving Christ when he cares for his wife and children. A parish worker has a change of heart and shows mercy to someone in need. A son commits himself to praying for his father. A woman discerns an invitation to help others in a situation where most people would be tempted to turn inward.

These are some of the stories you'll read in this chapter—stories that show how the gospel points us outside ourselves and calls us to relieve the spiritual and physical needs of others. Is your own reading of Scripture leading you in this direction?

As you read these stories, pause from time to time. Ask the Holy Spirit to set your heart on fire with a burning love that reaches out to the whole world!

Think About It!

St. Catherine of Siena, one of the Church's greatest saints, combined a life of intense prayer with loving service to family and friends, popes and priests and, in a special way, to the poor, the imprisoned, and the sick. Her motivation came from what she said the Lord told her in a mystical vision: "I have placed you among your neighbors so that you can do for them what you cannot do for me—that is, so that you may love them without any expectation of thanks or profit."

Pray It!

Take a few minutes to think about your life in light of this verse: "We know love by this, that he laid down his life for us—and we ought to lay down our lives for one another" (1 John 3:16).

Holy Spirit, help me to imitate my Lord's selfless love. How shall I lay down my life in service today?

If a Brother Has Nothing to Wear
By Janice L. Smith
Medford, Massachusetts

*If a brother or sister is ill-clad and in lack of daily food, and
one of you says to them, "Go in peace, be warmed and filled,"
without giving them the things needed for the body, what does
it profit? So faith by itself, if it has no works, is dead.*
(James 2:15-17)

It was a cold, snowy winter's morning. I was the only person in the rectory office, where I worked as pastoral coordinator for the parish. With my coat still on, I answered the ringing telephone. The caller was a man looking for a handout. I recognized his voice and immediately wanted to ignore his request—personally, I refer to him as the "crazy alcoholic guy." On occasions when he has come to the door and I've been alone, I have not opened it, as his presence unsettles me.

Attempting to placate the caller, I told him that all such requests are handled through the St. Vincent de Paul Society and that the person he needed to speak with wasn't in. I explained that we keep no money in the rectory and give only food or vouchers. I said I would get the message to the person in charge and suggested that he call me back later.

The man told me that his name was Paul, that a voucher would be okay, and that he also needed a duffel bag, as all his clothes were wet. He said he would call back in an hour.

Although I did telephone the St. Vincent de Paul representative, I was unable to reach him, and so I just continued going about my business. A while later, when the telephone rang again, I figured it was probably Paul and chose not to answer. I let the machine pick up the call. I was not ignoring the phone.

I was, in fact, avoiding having to talk with Paul again.

During the next hour, he called repeatedly at five-minute intervals, sometimes leaving a message, other times calling collect and having the operator tell him there was no answer. Increasingly annoyed, I figured I'd better speak to Paul or he would just keep pestering me. I couldn't avoid answering the phone for the entire day!

Picking up the phone, I again attempted to appease and even dissuade him. "Yes, I did try to relay your message, but I couldn't get through.... Father isn't in today.... There's nothing more I can do for you.... Sorry."

The first twinge of conscience struck. I knew that if the pastor were in, he would personally give him food from his cupboard or money from his own pocket. I have often witnessed his acts of hospitality and generosity.

Paul said he was desperate—his clothes were wet and he was cold and he wasn't sure where he could wait, protected from the elements, until I was able to reach someone else. Frankly, I am embarrassed to admit my insensitive and self-centered response to his desperate plea. Out of my mouth came these words: "That's all I can do. Sorry. I'll keep trying to reach the St. Vincent de Paul person. Try and keep warm." Then I hung up.

Twinge number two struck hard. I recalled the words of James 2:15-17: "If a brother or sister is ill-clad and in lack of daily food, and one of you says to them, 'Go in peace, be warmed and filled,' without giving them the things needed for the body, what does it profit? So faith by itself, if it has no works, is dead."

Other Scripture passages came to mind. Paul was persistent, as was the widow in the gospel parable: "This widow keeps bothering me" (Luke 18:5). Jesus' words, "Blessed are the poor in spirit" resounded in my heart (Matthew 5:3)—Paul deserved to be humanely treated, with dignity. Tobit 4:7 says: "Give alms from your possessions.... Do not turn your face away from anyone who is poor, and the face of God will not be turned away from you."

I regretted my contradictory, even hypocritical response and experienced a change of heart. My external behavior and my internal disposition needed an immediate adjustment! I left the rectory, went home, and got an old duffel bag from my attic, groceries from my kitchen cabinet, and a ten-dollar bill from my "emergency fund." Placing these items in a paper shopping bag marked with Paul's name, I drove back to church and left the bag on a bench in the foyer.

When Paul called again, I told him where to find the bag. When he said "God *bless* you," my reply was "God bless *you!*" I didn't tell him I was the benefactor, nor did I tell anyone in the parish about our interactions. I must admit my main concern was that I would be chastised for giving someone money, which is against our policy.

One morning the following week, when I arrived for work, Paul was busily involved in an outdoor project. I was surprised to see him cleaning the front and side steps of the church, removing remnants of ice, snow, and residual sand. We exchanged greetings, and I asked him what he was up to. He told me that he was helping out, paying back, because we had been so kind to him the week before.

In reflecting on this incident, I am also reminded of the passage in Matthew 25:37-40:

Then the righteous will answer him, "Lord, when was it that we saw you hungry and gave you food, or thirsty and gave you something to drink? And when was it that we saw you a stranger and welcomed you, or naked and gave you clothing?…" And the king will answer them, "Truly, I tell you, just as you did it to one of the least of these who are members of my family, you did it to me."

A Psalm for Dad
By Paul Harvey
Urbana, Maryland

But I trusted in your steadfast love; my heart shall rejoice in your salvation. I will sing to the LORD, because he has dealt bountifully with me. (Psalm 13:5-6)

Dad had been essentially unemployed for about ten years. He had jobs here and there, but they never worked out. He had always come across as a very cheerful, confident man, but we watched his confidence erode as the years passed. Although he was a practicing Catholic, his church attendance seemed to offer him no real consolation. He knew none of the joy and peace that I and others had come to know in a personal relationship with Jesus.

I really wanted him to know what I knew and would often encourage him to pray and read his Bible. So would Mum. Poor Dad! These encouragements would generally be met with "Yes, I know I should," but then nothing would happen. He would continue to be burdened and weighed down—and we'd be exasperated!

One night I resolved to pray for my dad throughout the night. I only made it to about 2:00 a.m., but by that time I had received an answer and some direction.

I had been asking the Lord why Dad seemed unable to move on in his walk with him. The Lord gave me a sense that Dad had spiritual enemies who were working against him. He also gave me Psalm 13 as a Scripture passage to pray every day. I adapted it a bit, praying it for Dad like this:

How long, O LORD? Will you forget him forever?
How long will you hide your face from him?
How long must he bear pain in his soul,
and have sorrow in his heart all day long?
How long shall his enemy be exalted over him?

Consider and answer him, O LORD my God!
Give light to his eyes, or he will sleep the sleep of death,
and his enemy will say, "I have prevailed";
his foes will rejoice because he is shaken.

But I trusted in your steadfast love;
my heart shall rejoice in your salvation.
I will sing to the LORD,
because he has dealt bountifully with me.

I prayed this every night for over a year. Then, during Easter break in 1989, I was home from college and went out for a beer with Dad. Before we left I prayed for him, and the Lord put on my heart to pass along a message: "Tell him I just want him to pray to me five minutes a day." That was it. No pressure tactics. No urging and cajoling. No cost-benefit analysis. Just a simple message to pass on.

So there we were in the pub, and we had the best father-son time I can remember. I shared with Dad about the Lord's work in my own life. He was smiling and seemed to enjoy listening to me. Then I passed on the message to him and told him that God wanted him to know that he was his son.

After that, Dad did begin to pray and read his Bible. In a letter he sent me when I was back at college, he passed on a bit of financial advice and then wrote, "By the way, I am praying for five minutes every day ... at least!" Also, at long last, he got a job that he enjoyed. We began to see some of his old confidence return.

One morning around this time, as I began to pray my usual Psalm 13 for Dad, I sensed the Lord saying, "You don't need to pray it any more. I've answered it." So I began to thank God every night instead.

On May 20, 1989, a couple of months after that chat with Dad over a beer, I was awakened by a phone call. It was Mum, calling with the news that Dad had passed away the previous night. The day before he died, she said, he had attended a prayer meeting. Someone commented to Mum afterward: "He looked so happy!"

> But I trusted in your steadfast love;
> my heart shall rejoice in your salvation.
> I will sing to the LORD,
> because he has dealt bountifully with me.

Jesus Knocking at the Door
By Sr. Thérèsia Murata
Himeji City, Japan

Prepare the way of the Lord, make his paths straight. (Luke 3:4)

Three strong taps! The first one came during Advent 1948—a voice from within that brought the message: "Make his paths straight" (Luke 3:4). Was this an invitation to become a religious sister? A second strong tap came when I received a letter from abroad; it was from my elementary school teacher, whom I had not seen since childhood. She wrote:

To everyone there is a high way and a low way,
And everyone should choose his or her way to go!

To me, a spoiled young person with little initiative, this Catholic nun had written a personal word! It launched my second journey of inquiry. Finally, the third tap, in the words of a minister who had been invited to address the assembly on the day of my graduation. The auditorium was quiet, and then he spoke: "'Enter through the narrow gate' (Matthew 7:13), before your load becomes too heavy to make a turn!"

My eyes opened wide, and my confidence in the Lord grew. These three taps seemed to make sense of my life. As I reflected on them, I knew that they were three gradual steps by which the loving Lord led me to decide to become a religious sister dedicated to teaching young people.

Was God giving me a part to play in building his kingdom? There was certainly a lot of building to do in my country at that time. Japan had lost everything after World War II! I remember how poor we Japanese were. We were poor both physically and spiritually. We had lost hope in the future. Our traditions and history—all had to be rethought and rewritten. There was to be no more cult of the imperial family, no more ancestor worship. We had to learn how to utilize the great gift of freedom which had been newly bestowed on us. Many people had fought for freedom, but we had yet to learn its true value.

At that time, about fifty years ago, a large number of Japanese were converting to Christianity. I found myself questioning whether the conversions were genuine. Were these converts hoping for material advancement? Were they just looking for stronger leadership because so many traditional values had collapsed?

I was not reassured by what happened in a small village about an hour away from our convent. The whole place had been converted in no time by a Belgian priest who made friends with one of the village leaders. With much kindness, he had led the townspeople to be baptized. The village leader's daughter even became a nun. However, after some time, one after another of the new converts left the Church and returned to their former way of life.

I wondered: Was there anything I could do to help my people to know Christ and become really Christian in their hearts?

One day, during the period when I was teaching and receiving training to become a Presentation of Mary sister, the Belgian priest approached me for advice. He wanted my ideas on how to utilize a large sum of money that he had received for mission work. I knew that in other countries there was Christian literature designed for children who had little or no access to religious education. I suggested, "How about publishing pamphlets for children who know nothing about Christ's existence?" Without a moment's hesitation, the priest replied, "Put together the first issue!"

So I did. Because the film *Bambi* was popular in Japan at that time, I named the pamphlet *Kojika,* which means "little deer." A local printer quickly prepared it for distribution, and soon the pamphlet was known all over the country. Even now it is still popular among children who attend Sunday school.

Fifty years have passed quickly. I am now retired from teaching, but I still keep in contact with my former students. Not too long ago, one of them helped me with another evangelistic idea. Together, we were able to launch a local telephone-sermon service, which is generously sponsored by church funding. Callers hear a three-minute talk by a priest. The sermons are easy to understand and contain practical advice. Many people who are lonely or sick never let a day pass without listening to these sermons. Even non-Christians can enjoy them! This type of outreach already existed in other parts of Japan, but our city now has the largest listening audience.

But this is no time to rest from our labors. The world is changing. The pursuit of personal wealth has gotten in the way of choosing the narrow gate into God's kingdom. There seem to be fewer adult baptisms. I regret to see that some of my former students who are filled with faith and love for Christ are finding it difficult to obtain their family's permission to get baptized.

As I keep asking the Lord to show me how to build his kingdom, I continue to utter the prayer of Venerable Charles de Foucauld: "No matter what happens, the Father's love is so strong, and his will is done." And as I ponder our low number of converts, I seem to hear my fourth tapping: "Prepare the way of the Lord, make his paths straight"!

Written with the assistance of Lesley Crowe-Delaney.

My Cancer and My Call
By Kathy Ann Rogers
Gibraltar, Michigan

I am with you always. (Matthew 28:20)

Six years ago, I felt a lump in my left breast and decided to consult my doctor. At that point, I was not concerned about cancer. I was only forty-one and in generally good health, and there was no history of breast cancer in my family.

One doctor examined me, then called in a second doctor. They left the room without saying anything, and then returned to say that they were referring me to a more specialized cancer center in the area. Although they said there was a 95 percent chance that I did not have cancer, I was concerned. I immediately started to pray.

Trying to stay calm, I drove to the cancer center. X rays were taken, and I was asked to wait for the results. They were disturbing. Something had shown up on the mammogram, the doctor told me, and they wanted to do a biopsy right away. I was instructed to eat a light lunch and come back in an hour. On my way out, I stopped to call my cousin and have my name added to her personal prayer list.

I got back to the cancer center with a little time to spare. Noticing a chapel, I went in and crashed. As I sat there in the back row, I started crying harder and harder. Then, from deep within my heart, I heard a voice that said, "Do not be afraid, for I am with you always." An immediate calmness rushed over me, even as I came to the realization that I did have cancer. The voice went on to assure me that I would survive and that somehow the experience would work for the good. "Trust me." I whispered "okay" and left for the biopsy.

Later, as I discussed this experience with my husband, we both had the sense that God was going to use my illness to help others. It struck me that this was an honor. I wasn't rich or famous, and I didn't know exactly what to do. Even so, I had been chosen by God to actually help someone! Although I was anxious about the biopsy results, I was ready to take on whatever task was at hand.

I was not really surprised when the results confirmed the presence of a malignant tumor. A mastectomy seemed to be the best option, and I had surgery on May 5, 1997. The doctor was pleased with the results and said that my chances for complete recovery were excellent. Full of gratitude, I thought back to my encounter with God in the chapel. It was as the mysterious voice had indicated: the cancer had been large enough to be detected but small enough to be cured.

Many people knew that I had cancer, and it wasn't long before I got a phone call. Even as I was recovering from surgery, a cousin asked if I could talk to one of her coworkers who had discovered a lump in her breast. Here I was, propped up in bed and unable to use my left arm, talking on the phone to a very frightened woman. I answered her questions as best I could, assured her that God would take care of her, and encouraged her to trust him.

About this time, a realization came to me: *This is what God wants me to do!* I have always joked about having the gift of gab. I have no problem talking to people I don't know—to me, a stranger is only a friend that I have never met. And especially since I believe that fear is based on lack of knowledge, neither have I felt reluctant to talk about my cancer. Now I understood that God was asking me to put these gifts together and use them in his name.

I have now been cancer free for over six years. During that time, I have talked about cancer and God to church groups, women's groups, friends, relatives, and anybody else who will listen. I have helped raise people's consciousness of the importance of breast cancer research and of early detection. (I was especially proud when a friend called one day to thank me for having given his wife the courage to get her first mammogram.) As part of my effort to encourage other women with breast cancer, I recently became a counselor in the American Cancer Society's "Reach for Recovery" program.

Through it all, I still rely on Jesus' promise: "I am with you always."

My Little Loaf and Fish
By Lisa Levy
Port Byron, Illinois

Jesus asked them, "How many loaves have you?" They said, "Seven, and a few small fish." (Matthew 15:34)

Sometimes I feel so overwhelmed by the hurt, evil, and tragedies of this world. Often I ask God what he wants me to do to help. Then I think—what can I do? I am only one person. Time and time again, however, God gently reminds me that he doesn't ask me to carry the weight of the world on my shoulders. That is his job. Our loving Father simply asks me to love one person at a time.

In the aftermath of the September 11 terrorist attacks, as the holidays approached, I felt especially overwhelmed and anxious. With five children, holidays are exciting but very busy. And because of the economic downturn related to 9/11, I had to return to work part time. My heart also ached for the people who had been directly affected by the events of September 11. I could empathize. My brother flies for a major airline. Two family friends died in the World Trade Center towers. My father-in-law used to work on Wall Street, close to Ground Zero. My husband works in finance and is from Long Island. A dear friend lives in Washington, D.C.

Christmas is a time to prepare and renew our hearts for the coming of the Savior. Yet how could I do that, in the aftermath of such horrifying and frightening events?

My answer came so clearly, early one December morning. As I read the Mass readings for that day—specifically Matthew 15:29-37, which includes the story of Jesus feeding the multitudes with loaves and fish—I felt a rush of excitement and insight.

Jesus' disciples asked him, "Where are we to get enough bread in the desert to feed so great a crowd?" I agreed with the disciples. "I'm so overwhelmed, Father," I prayed. "How can I do all this work?"

"Jesus asked them, 'How many loaves have you?' They said, 'Seven, and a few small fish.'" I continued to pray: "I don't have a bully pulpit or wealth or power, Lord. What can I do?"

"Then ordering the crowd to sit down on the ground, he took the seven loaves and the fish; and after giving thanks he broke them and gave them to the disciples, and the disciples gave them to the crowds. And all of them ate and were filled."

I next read the day's commentary from *The Word Among Us* and was astounded. The meditation said that *we* are to bring Jesus our little portion of faith, love, and courage, and that he supernaturally multiplies our resources so that we have

enough—no matter how many people we encounter, no matter how difficult the challenges we face.

"Yes Lord!" I exclaimed. "I hear you! Yes! You are telling
me to fully rely on you. If I come with an open heart, you will
direct me, guide me, and provide in abundance. Thank you,
Father! You are indeed in charge, and we are not alone!"

The commentary continued with Mother Teresa's statement:
"I never look at the masses. I look only at the individual. I can
only love one person at a time. Just begin: one, one, one...."
I prayed: "I can do that, Father. I can love one person at a time.
I give you the hurt, loss, and destruction of this world. I will
receive and reflect your love here and now right where I am.
I can do that!"

Then came the clincher. I was so excited as I read: "*Trust
Jesus to multiply the little you offer your friends or family....
Don't be afraid to tell others how prayer helps you make it
through even the hardest day or how reading the Bible has lifted
your burdens....*" I felt that God was giving me the biggest hug
ever! Bible study and prayer ministry are near and dear to my
heart.

"Thank you, Father! Thank you! You are an awesome God!
Thank you for speaking to me through your word. Thank you
for taking away my grief and worry. Take my little loaf and fish
and use me. Holy Spirit, mold me and teach me how to love.
I place my worries and concerns in your hands. Jesus, please
abundantly bless all those who are hurting from evils in the
world. I love you, Father. Amen!"

Once again, God had showed me how deeply he loves us and
how much he desires to give us the strength and perseverance
that come from him. I felt renewed and encouraged, ready to
move forward toward our Savior's coming. Later that day, I
shared my early morning revelation with a friend. She was

renewed and inspired, too, and eager to give Jesus her loaf and fish.

Since then, I have been especially focused on trying to act as the Holy Spirit nudges me—perhaps by encouraging someone with a card or phone call or by spending extra time with them. Whatever I do, I wish to be an instrument of God's love and grace with my little loaf and fish.

A High Calling in Everyday Clothes
By Jeff Pirrung
Jacksonville, Florida

Truly I tell you, just as you did it to one of the least of these who are members of my family, you did it to me.
(Matthew 25:40)

In his parable about the final judgment, Jesus said that people will be given or denied entry into eternal life on the basis of how they treated him. The "sheep" in his parable are surprised by this. "Lord, when did we see you hungry and feed you, or thirsty and give you drink? When did we see you a stranger and welcome you, or naked and clothe you? When did we see you ill or in prison and visit you?"

I for one am glad the sheep asked these questions, because Jesus' answer helps me see how to serve him in my own life: Whatever you did for one of these least brothers of mine, you did for me.

Over time, I have discovered that I have many opportunities to minister to Jesus by helping his "least brothers." This is especially true at home, where my wife Denise and I are busy caring for our four beautiful daughters: Kathryn, eight; Leone, four; Mary, two; and Caroline, three months. I've come to believe that when I respond to their needs out of love for Christ, I really am building up the Church and living out my call to serve Jesus.

Often, though, this high calling looks and feels anything but exalted. Take this typical evening, for example. Denise has gone out for the evening for a meeting at the parish, leaving me with our four girls, and with the hopes that I'll get to catch the football game on television.

Caroline, the newborn, fusses, starts to cry, and then wails unmercifully. Mom will be gone for at least two more hours. What do I do? Instinctively, I pick up this helpless little angel and rock her back and forth. Slowly, she regains composure. Soon she is content and cooing.

Then suddenly, I hear Mary, who has been asleep for half an hour. "Joo-Joo! Joo-Joo!" she is yelling at the top of her lungs. Decision time: How do I keep Caroline content while attending to Mary's cries for apple juice? Do I take her with me on the mission and risk her getting unsettled? Or do I put her down? Both options appear less than appealing. I take the first risk, with no bad consequences. Mary takes two tiny drinks and fades off into a deep sleep. Time to get back to reading Leone her goodnight story, which I'm squeezing in between math quizzes with Kathryn.

In the back of my mind, the "big game" is still lurking, along with my hopes of a solid chunk of time in front of the TV. But first, I have a to-do list I want to get through. I finish Leone's goodnight story, help her get her pajamas on, get her a drink, say prayers, sing two verses of "Silent Night"—"like Mommy does"—and one verse of "Away in a Manger," which I am reproachfully told I sing "too loud." Another daughter down and sleeping for the night.

Kathryn and I finish her studies, then do the dishes and clean the kitchen together. We talk about some trouble she has been having with two kids in her class. We put together a plan that should alleviate some of the problems. I kiss her goodnight, say prayers, and tuck her in. It's 9:30. Finally, all my daughters are in bed. I straighten up the living room and am about to turn on the vacuum cleaner (the last item on my list), when I hear Caroline wailing again. Denise said to give her a bottle if she seemed hungry, so I mix up the formula.

As I'm feeding Caroline, I hear Mary toss and turn and then cry—probably nightmares. I call for her, as I can't move easily from the couch. But, for the first time in her life, Mary decides that she will obey the rule of staying in her bed after being put down for the night—and she keeps crying. As soon as I can, I lay Caroline down and go to Mary. She calms down and is drifting back to sleep, so I attempt to slip out of the room. She catches me in the act, and I am busted—her trust is shattered. "I'll be right back," I assure her, and go get the baby. When I return, Mary insists that I crawl into bed with her.

The door opens, and a feeling of peace comes over me. My wife, the love of my life, has returned. Now everything will settle down. But I meet Denise at the door and find her in tears. Quickly, I realize that my night isn't over yet. We engage in deep conversation on topics that came up at her parish meeting, on our need to make decisions guided by the teaching of Christ and the Church, and on the fact that secular teaching guides so many decisions made in our world—and sometimes even in our parish. Soon it is 11:00, and I am exhausted.

I fall fast asleep. At 2:25 a.m., I wake up to find Leone in our bed. "Daddy, I don't have enough room," she says. I tell her to go get her pillow and blanket and sleep on the floor. "Or go back to your bed." Leone is disappointed and doesn't understand, but I insist. In the long term, the family will benefit if I get some sleep.

I wake up about 6:00 a.m. to catch "Sports Center." I see that the game I had wanted to watch was a blowout and not really worth the time anyway. I make breakfast, get ready for work, and head off for another day at the office.

Much of my life is like that evening. For the most part, I have no big-time sufferings or calls to exceptional heroism. But I have discovered that, in their own way, the ordinary interruptions, irritations, and annoyances of daily life can also be effective training in dying to yourself and laying down your life for others.

As I struggle to do this each and every day, with the Lord's grace and love, it is the big perspective that keeps me going: Whatever you did for one of these least brothers of mine, you did for me.

8

Help When You Need It

Here is a selection of "just in time" stories that highlight God's intervention in the lives of his people. May they strengthen your faith that a loving God is with you both in ordinary times and at critical moments. May they encourage you to turn to him for peace, protection, insight, comfort, and all the other riches in his spiritual treasury.

And speaking of treasuries, notice that a couple of these stories highlight the importance of "stocking up" on God's word. Rosemarie Hunt writes that her lifelong habit of reading and studying Scripture has provided her with "a mental storeroom" of passages that can serve as "life preservers in a stormy sea." Dianne Spotts took her Bible along on a weekend camping trip and worked on memorizing a psalm—which turned out to be just the right prayer for the week that followed.

What about you? Is it time to build yourself a "storeroom" of Scripture? Or, if you already have one, are you keeping it well stocked?

Think About It!

How often we forget about all the "just in time" moments when God has provided for a special need! Identify one or several of those moments in your own life, and take a few minutes to thank God for them now. Talk to the Lord about what you might do to saturate your mind more thoroughly in

Scripture. Ask the Holy Spirit to improve your memory (see John 14:26)!

Pray It!

I cried out, "Lord, you are my Father;
do not forsake me in the days of trouble....
I will praise your name continually,
and will sing hymns of thanksgiving."
My prayer was heard, for you saved me from destruction
and rescued me in time of trouble.
For this reason I thank you and praise you,
and I bless the name of the Lord. (Sirach 51:10-12)

Deliver Us from Evil
By Helen Bloodgood
Jupiter, Florida

Our Father who art in heaven,
Hallowed be thy name.... (Matthew 6:9)

It was two days before Thanksgiving. I had just finished buying groceries and was loading them into my car in the supermarket parking lot, taking pains to arrange a party cake and some flowers carefully on the back seat. I got in my car, started the engine, and went to lock my doors. Suddenly, from out of nowhere, a man jumped into the rear seat, grabbed me by the neck, and demanded that I start driving.

I was completely taken by surprise. Confused thoughts raced through my mind. *Is this a joke? A dream? Are they filming a movie here?* But this was no joke, dream, or movie. Even now, I can hardly find the words to express the horror and terror that seized me as I realized that I was being abducted.

Stunned and scared, I tried to persuade the man to let me go and take my car and jewelry instead. I might have saved my breath. "If you don't drive," he said in a cold, hard voice, "I have a gun and I'll blow your brains out."

I put my car into reverse as his grip tightened around my neck. He demanded that I drive south on U.S. Highway 1. I started to pray silently. Just that morning, thinking it odd but feeling compelled, I had put a picture of my twenty-year-old daughter on my key chain. Looking at it now as it swung from the ignition, I found even more reasons for prayer: *God, thank you so much for letting it be me and not her. But please, let me live for her!* I kept watching her beautiful face and smile, and it was as though she was urging me, "Live! Live!" I didn't know it then, but God was giving me courage and the will to survive.

What did this intruder want? I feared the worst. Thinking about how to escape, I drove twenty-five miles below the speed limit in hopes that someone would notice. Passing a parking lot, I looked for a police car I had sometimes seen there. When these attempts failed, I headed for a nearby police station. Before I could get there, however, the man ordered me to turn into the parking lot of a dimly lit shopping center. Then he demanded that I pull into the back alley. "No, I won't go there with you," I said and kept driving to the front of the old shopping center. But when I saw how dead and deserted it looked, my heart sank.

The man told me to stop the car, and I hoped against hope that he'd just get out and leave. But he went into a rage. "You've done nothing that I asked you to do!" he shouted and proceeded to strangle me. I grabbed his hands and desperately struggled to break his grip as I realized what was happening: *He's trying to kill me by breaking my neck!* A bolt of pain shot up my neck and head, but somehow I managed to press my head so hard into the headrest that he couldn't grab and twist it. My strength could only have come from God. He then hit me a couple of times, dragged me into the back seat by my head and hair, and attempted to violate me sexually.

I fought my attacker for close to twenty minutes, which seemed like an eternity. I prayed silently to God the entire time—*Please help me. Please help me.* Finally, it looked like my demise was near. Crouched on top of me, brandishing a full bottle of liquor over my head, he announced, "I'm going to kill you now. You're a dead woman."

As a child, I had been taught that I should pray the Act of Contrition at the time of death. I remember considering it, but what came to my lips at that moment was the *Our Father*. I started to pray it out loud.

"Shut up!" my attacker screamed. I invited him to pray with me.

"It's too late for me," he said.

I told him it is never too late with God. And again I began, "Our Father, who art in heaven...."

The man was furious and began shouting horrendous profanities. "I told you to shut up! I'm going to kill you!"

"Well then," I told him, "I can go any way that I want. And I'm going to go praying." Pain was engulfing my entire beaten body. With no strength left to fight, I knew I was going to die. I closed my eyes then and prepared to meet my dear God and Creator. I began to pray the *Our Father*—softly now—for the third time.

How can I describe what happened next? All of a sudden, the terror and physical pain I was experiencing simply vanished. I felt bathed in warmth and light, and a sense of peace flooded my whole being. It was the most beautiful thing I had ever experienced. *So this is the way it feels to die!* I felt an inexpressible joy as I continued to pray and waited for the blow to hit.

But nothing happened. Suddenly I felt the weight of my attacker's body lifting off mine. I opened my eyes to find him sitting up with his head in his hands, trembling. In a flash, two realizations came to me—that I had been delivered by God through prayer and saving grace, and that the cake and flowers I had placed in the back seat were a complete mess!

"Look what you did! You ruined my celebration!"

Somehow, my rebuke changed the whole tone of things. We

got into a conversation. My assailant told me his first name, what city he lived in, and that he had been on heroin for six days. He asked me to drive him back to the parking lot where he had jumped into my car. By this time, incredible pain was coursing through my body again, but I drove and kept talking to get his attention off me.

When we got to the supermarket, he told me to park in the last space at the darkest end of the lot. I offered to take him to a hospital or call for help with my cell phone. He refused, afraid that I would alert the police.

Dear Jesus, how will I ever get this man out of my car? Fearful of another attack, I prayed silently. *Please deliver me.* Suddenly it came to me that I might offer to walk him across the highway so that he could make his getaway. He agreed. Painfully, I walked with him to the median, still his prisoner as he held on to me tightly. He started across the other half of the highway—heading right into traffic—and I quickly pulled him back. "You're going to get yourself killed," I warned. I also said I was going no further than across the road and that he must let me go there.

"Why are you being so nice to me?" he said as we got to the other side. I looked him straight in the face and said, "I feel very sorry for you. And I'm going to pray for you." He released his grip, and I turned and ran back to my car. Once inside, I went into shock. Finally, I managed to call my husband.

I sustained serious injuries from the attack—four badly damaged discs in my neck and multiple contusions and bruises to my head, jaw, and ribs. But as I rode to the hospital with my husband and daughter, I felt deliriously joyful. I knew that I had experienced nothing short of a miracle. I felt so loved and special to God! I thanked and praised him again and again for saving my life.

I kept praying the *Our Father*, and every time I came to "forgive those who trespass against us," I would hesitate. Suddenly I felt the Spirit speaking to my soul, telling me I must forgive my attacker. Without hesitation I responded: "Dear God, you love this man as much as you love me. He is as much a child of yours as I am. I forgive him. Please forgive him."

From that day forward, I prayed for my assailant. Instead of taking drugs for pain and anxiety, I prayed. This heartfelt forgiveness and continuous prayer for him and his family brought a certain joy and peace into my heart and spirit. God gave me the strength to heal and go on with my life. Even my doctors were amazed at my progress through therapy.

But I won't pretend that I've had an easy recovery. To this day, I live in pain. My physical injuries have affected my work as a fitness instructor and seamstress. And even though I experienced God's presence and protection during the assault, fears and nightmares pursued me for a long time afterward. Even now, not one day goes by that I do not recall the experience.

Eight months later, the man who attacked me was finally captured (after sexually assaulting a child). Only then was I finally able to cry—and to realize that I needed professional counseling for Post Traumatic Stress Syndrome.

I cannot change what happened to me. I can never go back to the way life was the day before my attack. Sometimes I wonder if I would want to, for God has drawn so much good out of this evil! My husband and I both had a chance to talk to my assailant at his sentencing; he knows he is forgiven and that we pray for him. Also, the attack, trial, and sentencing were highly profiled by the media, with every story mentioning the "miracle," the *Our Father*, and the power of prayer. Doors have opened, giving me numerous opportunities to speak about prayer and forgiveness. I've also had the opportunity to meet with other women who have been sexually assaulted or abused.

My daughter has changed, too. I have seen her blossom into a young woman who never seems to tire in her courageous, unselfish desire to help others. She has formed a charitable organization—Women on Watch—whose mission is to teach women basic principles of awareness and self-defense and to provide funding for DNA testing in rape cases. She has been trained as a counselor with the National Organization for Victim Assistance. Together, she and I have helped educate police departments on how to treat assault victims. With God's continued grace, our family has been brought closer together in our efforts to help others.

All this has given me a new mission in life—to work for the prevention and survival of violent assault, as well as for DNA testing so that predators can be captured and victims can learn to live again. Most of all, I want to proclaim the greatness of our God and give testimony to the power of prayer and the awesome grace of God's healing through forgiveness. How good our Father is!

Pitch Your Tent on God's Word
By Dianne Spotts
Hatfield, Pennsylvania

You, LORD, are all I have, and you give me all I need;
my future is in your hands.
(Psalm 16:5, Today's English Version)

A long weekend of camping at Hickory Run State Park could be the "R & R" I need, I thought. It was the "sandwich" season of my life, and I felt pressed between deep concern for my aging parents and raising three teenagers and an eleven-year-old. My dad's health had been deteriorating steadily. Thankfully, my children were healthy—and active, testing their limits and mine. Stress and worry were my constant companions.

A few days away with my husband sounded terrific, although I did have doubts about his plans to go tenting in the woods. However, he made me some promises: If I agreed to camp out, he promised that we would have a great campsite near a clean bathhouse with hot showers, that he would do all the cooking, and that he would bring me a comfy cot. After checking the weather forecast and making arrangements for the children, I agreed to give it a try.

I packed a good book, a Bible, some note paper, and a prayer card that contained Scripture verses from Psalm 16. Some of my Protestant friends inspired me with their ability to quote from the Bible, so I decided to try memorizing these few verses while I was away.

Waking up on our first morning to the smell of coffee perking and bacon sizzling sealed the deal! After cleaning up the breakfast dishes, I read one of the verses over and over, closing my eyes periodically to repeat it from memory: "You, LORD, are all I have, and you give me all I need; my future is in your hands."

We took an invigorating three-hour walk, which involved scaling a small mountain to arrive at a breathtaking view of the Lehigh River. From that vantage point, we saw some adventurous people white-water rafting. Back to our campsite for lunch, relaxing, and repeating my study of the next verses: "How wonderful are your gifts to me, how good they are! I praise the LORD because he guides me and in the night my conscience warns me" (verses 6-7).

We spent the rest of our afternoon quietly, by a gurgling brook. We were serenaded by a choir of birds under perfect skies. "I am always aware of the LORD's presence; he is near and nothing can shake me" (verse 8).

Our weekend continued blissfully, as I communed with nature and God through his word. On our last day, while we were packing, I also covered: "And so I am thankful and glad, and feel completely secure…. You will show me the path of life, your presence fills me with joy and brings me pleasure forever" (verses 9, 11).

When we arrived home, all hell broke loose! My dad was taken to the hospital, and another serious family problem developed. I could hardly think, I could hardly pray—except for the psalm verses newly stored inside me. As I repeated them over and over, I received great ministry from the living Word of God—because bit by little bit, I believed what I was saying.

Our good Lord gave me what I needed before I needed it. "You, Lord, are all I have, and you give me all I need; my future is in your hand."

The Angel and the Serpent
By Patricia Cutie
Beaufort, South Carolina

For he will give his angels charge of you
to guard you in all your ways. (Psalm 91:11)

My parents always told me that each of God's children receives a very special gift from him at birth: their very own guardian angel to protect them from harm. As a child, I loved saying the well-known prayer: "Angel of God, my guardian dear, to whom God's love commits me here. Ever this day be at my side, to light and guard, to rule and guide." When I grew older, however, I fell away from this practice. Not until many years later was my devotion to my guardian angel rekindled. The reawakening began nearly ten years ago, on one of those sweltering South Carolina days.

"I need to go for a swim!" I decided. Putting on my bathing suit, I headed for the swimming pool in the backyard. My husband had gone fishing, so I had the whole afternoon. I walked down the steps into the pool. It was great. The water temperature was 84° F—perfect, since I love to swim in warm water.

But as I was about to push off from the side of the pool, the strangest thing happened. I felt a jolt to my left shoulder. It was so strong that it stopped me instantly. Then from within me, a voice said, "Get out of the water at once! There is great danger! Don't waste a minute!" The warning was so forceful that I was out of the pool in a flash.

"What was all that about?" I wondered as I stood on the deck. I checked the pool skimmers: they were clean, except for a few leaves. I walked around the deck, looking down into the pool. Then something caught my eye. In an instant, my puzzlement vanished and my heart started pounding, for there in the water was a slithering eighteen-inch snake. I am deathly afraid of snakes, and to think that I had almost swum with one just blew my mind.

Feeling weak, I sat down and reflected on what had happened. That jolt to my left shoulder and that inner voice telling me to get out of the water—surely, the warnings had come from my guardian angel! For the first time in years, my angel had my attention.

I was much too nervous to scoop the snake out of the pool with a net, so when a friend of my husband's stopped by a few hours later, I asked if he could do it for me. "No problem," he said. It took him a few tries to net the snake, which kept aggressively raising its head and striking out. Finally succeeding, he dropped the creature to the ground and killed it with a blow from a shovel. When that snake stopped slithering, we were both relieved.

To my amazement, when I told my husband's friend about my close encounter, his response confirmed my suspicion that I had been protected. "You are one lucky lady," he said. "Your guardian angel was looking after you and may have saved your life. That was a water moccasin—a very dangerous snake."

I'll never forget that experience. I now pray to my guardian angel every day and make a point of recommending this devotion to others. Finally, as I have reflected on the extraordinary gift of a guardian angel, Psalm 91 has acquired a new and special meaning.

> No evil shall befall you,
> no scourge come near your tent.
> For he will give his angels charge of you
> to guard you in all your ways.
> On their hands they will bear you up,
> lest you dash your foot against a stone.
> You will tread on the lion and the adder,
> the young lion and the serpent
> you will trample under foot. (Psalm 91:10-13)

A Love Letter from God
By Bruce Johnson
Grand Rapids, Michigan

O LORD, you have searched me and known me. (Psalm 139:1)

"The Bible," I was told when I was brand new to faith, "is a series of love letters from God to his people." One of the characteristics of cherished words from someone who loves us is that they always seem to know just what to say to us when we are going through something hard, even if we can't quite express what it is we're going through ourselves. That was certainly the case with me when I first came across Psalm 139, one of those "love letters from God."

I was only twenty, and it was less than a year since I had first heard God calling me closer to himself. He had already done a number of spectacular things for me. He had shown me that I had to love and cherish those around me more. He let me know how much he loved me and how I could bring his love to others, and then he gave me enough incredible experiences to fill a lifetime.

But like many new converts and other Christians who find God moving in their lives, I discovered that the devil does not sit idly by when he sees God working. I began to be plagued by temptations—some of them loathsome—and worse, by a sense that the devil was trying to woo me to himself. This experience was totally unfamiliar and, unlike my new experiences of God, it was oppressive and seemingly impossible to handle. I didn't give in to the temptations, but they put clouds in front of the sun. I worried that if they continued, I would get so worn down that I might give in. Then one afternoon I picked up my Bible.

I happened to open to Psalm 139. I had never read it before and was not looking for anything in particular, not even for a special timely word from God to me. My Bible simply happened to open to this page. As soon as I began to read, I was comforted, strengthened, and filled with wonder.

O LORD, you have searched me and known me.
You know when I sit down and when I rise up;
you discern my thoughts from far away. (verses 1-2)

God knew what was going on with me! He knew, in the smallest and most intimate details. Even more than knowing, he understood. Nothing went on with me that he did not see— and more clearly than I could see any movie I might be watching. I had known this to be true, but these words brought it home to me as never before.

As I read on, it got better. "Where can I go from your spirit? Or where can I flee from your presence?" the psalmist asked (verse 7). And the answer came back: absolutely nowhere!

If I take the wings of the morning
and settle at the farthest limits of the sea,
even there your hand shall lead me,
and your right hand shall hold me fast. (verses 9-10)

Even the way the psalmist expressed this truth had special meaning to me. The summer before, I had left my parents' home in England and hiked with my brother across glaciers in Norway. Now I was in the United States, still a long way from home. In all of these places, Christ had been very close, and I had felt his presence.

But it got better yet—the psalmist made it clear that even my darkest fears were lit up by the searching and saving light of God: "If I say, 'Surely the darkness shall cover me, and the light around me become night,' even the darkness is not dark to you; the night is as bright as the day" (verses 11-12). I felt much better—better still, as I read about God's greatness revealed in the vastness of his thoughts and plans.

Even so, that plaguing, gnawing uneasiness about the evil one who wouldn't leave me alone was in the back of my mind. But then I came to the end of the psalm: this too was understood. In words that could have been mine, the psalmist prayed:

O that you would kill the wicked, O God,
and that the bloodthirsty would depart from me—
those who speak of you maliciously,
and lift themselves up against you for evil!
Do I not hate those who hate you, O LORD?
And do I not loathe those who rise up against you?
I hate them with perfect hatred;
I count them my enemies. (verses 19-22)

And then came a prayer that was both a plea I felt sure would be heard and a triumphant statement of confidence that it would be answered. The psalm that had become my very own prayer ended:

Search me, O God, and know my heart;
test me and know my thoughts.
See if there is any wicked way in me,
and lead me in the way everlasting. (verses 23-24)

It wasn't just that the words "spoke to my condition," as people sometimes say, or gave me intellectual explanations of how God would take care of me. My encounter with Psalm 139 went far beyond that. It was the kind of experience you have when you are trembling with fear and someone puts their arms around you and whispers, "I understand," in a way that makes you believe it.

Almost three thousand years before, someone had written words that I myself could have written that very afternoon to express not just what was happening to me, but exactly how I felt about it! My state of mind, feelings, and anguish were not unknown to God. Without belittling or making light of them, he had taken them seriously and answered them on their own terms. And woven into this understanding was the assurance of God's faithfulness to see me through it all.

My fears did not melt away completely, and the temptations did not stop at once. They soon eased, however—and even before they did, I had a new confidence. I knew that I was not facing them alone. I was facing them with someone who understood them, who was stronger than they were, and who understood me. Furthermore, he cared about me so much that he inspired words that spoke precisely to my need, long before I was born.

God sent me a love letter when I needed it most. And with the sixth sense that lovers have, he sent me exactly the words I needed right then. My prayer for you is that whenever you face a need, you too will find your own "love letter" somewhere in the Bible and that it will bring you the assurance that God understands and cares deeply about your every circumstance. He will always see you through.

A Touch of the Master's Hand
By Merle Ankrum
West Fargo, North Dakota

The LORD *... inclined to me and heard my cry.*
He drew me up from the desolate pit....
He put a new song in my mouth,
a song of praise to our God. (Psalm 40:2-3)

Some people might describe their most precious moment in life as the day they were married or when their child was born. Others might say it was when they were elected to a public office or won the lottery. For me, this moment came following one of the most difficult times of my life.

With the exception of three years in the armed forces, I had spent my entire life on a ranch. My wife and I raised our six children in what I called the good life of being close to God and nature. I was also involved in numerous public service volunteer efforts. All of this made my life very fulfilling.

But at the age of fifty-seven, with our family raised, we made the decision to leave the ranch and seek new opportunities elsewhere. My wife went on ahead to look for work. Before joining her, I stayed behind for a short time to complete some unfinished business.

It was during this time that the heavy burden of loneliness, regret, anger, and sadness overwhelmed and nearly consumed me. Leaving the ranch was very difficult for me. I turned to prayer and reading the Bible, meditating on each passage of Scripture in search of answers and hope. They eluded me.

One day following this searching, I sank to the bottom of the pit. I could bear it no more, and my burden overwhelmed me. I remember crying out loud, "I can't take it any more!" In that instant, I believe I was shown what heaven must be like. The total burden was lifted from me. A peace and comfort beyond all imagining flooded my whole being, setting me free from all that was burdening me beyond my own ability to bear it.

Did God touch me? I have no doubt. Did I deserve for him to set me free? No. I know it happened only by his grace and love. I have had many low points in my life since then and have not felt this overwhelming love and peace again. Still, I never doubt that God is near to carry my greatest burdens.

This encounter with God left me wondering whether he reaches out this way to other desperate people who feel so completely empty and overwhelmed. I suspected and hoped that I was not alone in this experience of being lifted up and given a taste of heaven.

A few months later, we moved to Phoenix, Arizona, and found work. One Saturday morning, while waiting in the car as my wife did some shopping, I turned the radio on to a Christian program. A guest was testifying to God's great power and love. He had spent most of his life in prison, he said, and as time went by, this had become so great a burden that he found it impossible to bear. I listened with the greatest interest as he described what happened next. One day as he sat thinking of his past and feeling overwhelmed by hopelessness and despair, the man explained, he had stood up, thrown his hands in the air, and cried out, "I can't stand it any longer!" Then, in an instant, something had swept through and over him—a peace and calm that he had never, ever known before. Shortly after that, he was released from prison.

What other listeners were thinking as they listened to this broadcast, I don't know. As for me, I had the answer to my question. Yes, God does reach out to those who are in the "desolate pit"!

Along with this realization has come a change in the way I think about all those who are in prison. I feel much more compassion toward these men, women, and children. I ask myself, "What brought them to this point? Had they been abused? Were they unloved?" I try to remember to pray for them. Someday, I hope I will meet the prisoner who experienced the same wonderful miracle I did. Then he and I can rejoice together in this wonderful truth: No matter where or who we are, God is with us—always ready to pick us up and give us a touch of his hand, a foretaste of heaven.

Stocking Up
By Rosemarie Hunt
Avon, Connecticut

Every scribe who has been trained for the kingdom of heaven is like a householder who brings out of his treasure what is new and what is old. (Matthew 13:52)

The Scripture verse that has had the greatest impact on my life is Matthew 13:52. Both my grandmothers emphasized the importance of being familiar with the Old and the New Testaments. As a result, when I have faced periods of difficulty, I have had in my mental storeroom the Scripture passages that could become life preservers in a stormy sea. Here is a situation in which such passages may well have saved my life.

I lost my mother when I was three years old, and I did not have a happy childhood. Throughout my growing years, I planned for the day when I would have my own children. They would be wanted and loved; their needs would be uppermost in my mind. My older brother tried to discourage me, telling me that any children we might have would surely be "messed up" because of our difficult history. But I was certain I could protect my child from any fallout of my own childhood traumas.

When my son was born, however, it was immediately apparent that he was not the average baby. He was not comforted by being picked up and held; instead, he would stiffen and scream and throw himself backward. He slept only two or three hours at a time and spent his waking hours screaming. He had great difficulty digesting food, even when I was nursing him. The slightest change in his routine or any unexpected happening would throw him into screaming fits that could last for hours. Today, he would doubtless be diagnosed as having Asperger's Syndrome, but thirty-five years ago, no one had heard of that disorder.

When my son was an infant, people were sympathetic. By the time he was two, the general attitude was, "Why can't you handle that child?" Fortunately, my husband was very supportive. He was accepting of our son and patient with him, and he never blamed me for the difficulties we were facing. Together we consulted various experts, looking for an appropriate educational program. The experts disagreed on nearly everything except one point: As one educator put it, the major problem of a child who exhibited this kind of behavior was his mother.

I was overwhelmed with guilt and pain. Was I indeed responsible for all the problems my son was experiencing? If so, would he not be better off without me? I had begun to think of ways to kill myself when I turned to God in desperation. He gave me a very clear answer: "I shall not die, but I shall live, and recount the deeds of the LORD" (Psalm 118:17). Then I was reassured that my child needed me, and I knew that I could never desert him. I said this line over and over whenever I began to feel like I could not go on living. To let me know that he understood exactly how I was feeling, the Lord also gave me Psalm 69—part of which is seen as a description of his own Passion, but which is also a good description of despair.

How would I know the best things to do for my son? I doubted my ability to make the right choices, but again the Lord reassured me: "We know that all things work together for good for those who love God, who are called according to his purpose" (Romans 8:28). I knew he was telling me that I could trust him to oversee the results of my choices.

Even so, my doubts would not be stilled. After all, how could I qualify as one of "those who love God"? True love should be altruistic, self-sacrificing. It should put the loved one first. But when I came to God in prayer, it was *my* needs that were uppermost in my mind. Again God reassured me through Scripture: "Change and become like children" (Matthew 18:3). How does a little child love? Certainly not altruistically! Children are very self-centered, and their love is heavily tinged with self-interest. Yet this is hardly upsetting to the parents. When a little child tells them "I love you," no mother or father expects that love to be mature or self-sacrificing. A child's love is valued for what it is and is infinitely precious to the parents. Similarly, doesn't God understand our own weaknesses, self-centeredness, and immature attempts to love, and also find these attempts precious?

Reflecting on this, I had a vision of myself as a grimy child coming to my Father with a bedraggled bunch of dandelions. He accepts it with joy and places it in his finest crystal vase, because it is an offering from the child he loves. Once I was able to see myself as this beloved child, I could let go of my need to be the perfect mother. I placed my son in the Lord's care and trusted that he would bring good from my efforts. Gradually, he did.

The public school had no provision for a child like ours, but we were fortunate in finding a good parochial school that was willing to work with us. Our son graduated from parochial elementary and high school, spent three years in the Army, and graduated from college. He is now married and running his own business. He still has struggles with his essential personality, but he has learned to accept himself and to adjust to life's demands. Our son is a great joy to us, and every day I thank God for him and for the help we had raising him.

My experience has certainly confirmed me in daily Scripture study, and I recommend it to everyone. The more we have laid up in our mental "storehouse," the more easily the Lord can bring to mind the exact passage we need when we need it.

9

Afraid and Anxious No More

One of the contributors to this chapter observes that "an isolated Christian is a paralyzed Christian." You could say the same about a fearful, anxious Christian.

Food, clothing, health, work, violence, safety, the future, or death—whether we're worrying over big issues or small ones, over ourselves or those we love, anxiety is like a prison that keeps us from stepping out to do the work that God calls us to accomplish in the world.

Everyone struggles with anxiety and fear. The question is, what do we do with these natural feelings? How seriously do we take Jesus' repeated instructions not to worry or give in to fear (for example, Matthew 6:25, 31, 34)? That's something to ask yourself as you read through this chapter.

Think About It!

St. Thomas More didn't feel very brave as he sat imprisoned in the Tower of London. But during the weeks before his beheading in 1535, he found comfort in recalling that Jesus, too, had experienced fear (Mark 14:34). Thomas imagined Jesus addressing him as a "timid and peace-loving little sheep" and telling him what to do: "Be content to have me as your only shepherd, to follow me as your leader. Since you do not have confidence in yourself, hope in me. Look, I am walking ahead of you on this frightening road."

As it turned out, Thomas died bravely and joyfully, after light-heartedly asking the executioner to spare his beard!

Pray It!

Identify the situations that are making you feel especially worried and fearful right now. Let these Scripture verses encourage you to give them to God with complete confidence:

> Do not worry about anything, but in everything by prayer and supplication with thanksgiving let your requests be made known to God. And the peace of God, which surpasses all understanding, will guard your hearts and your minds in Christ Jesus. (Philippians 4:6-7)

> Cast all your anxiety on him, because he cares for you. (1 Peter 5:7)

Comfort in the City
By the Rev. Harriet E. Rodriguez
New York, New York

Comfort, O comfort my people,
says your God. (Isaiah 40:1)

It was my eldest son's thirty-second birthday, and my daughter-in-law was planning a celebration later on that evening. I could never have imagined how differently the day would turn out. It was September 11, 2001.

I live and work in New York City and was in the area when the first plane plunged into the Twin Towers. Huge, thick balls of smoke burst up into the sky. People were running, screaming for help, asking what was going on. Crowds of people were walking and running across the Brooklyn Bridge, seeking rides or trying to get home. The trains stopped running and buses were filled to capacity, many times refusing to stop at all.

I realized that I, too, had to find a way to get home. For a moment, though, I felt vulnerable and confused, like a sitting duck. Should I run or hide or remain at the bus stop? I started to pray, asking God for his guidance as crowds of people surged and pressed around me.

I began walking. As I did, I heard a report that both Twin Towers had collapsed and that the Pentagon had been attacked as well. *How could such a nice day turn out so mean and evil?* I asked myself. *Who is responsible?*

I worried about my family. Where were my sons and my daughter-in-law? Were they all safe? I thought about Jesus' words, too. I remembered how he said that the end of time would come without warning, with no time to get ready. I wondered if this was the day of his return.

As I continued to walk, an inner voice broke through my anxiety. It said, "Comfort ye my people." Suddenly I realized that I had to help or reach out in some way at this critical moment. With that thought came a peace such as I had never before experienced. I just knew that God would take care of me. Jesus and I had connected, and even though the city was in turmoil, I was no longer worried. Jesus would see me through.

I stopped off at a nearby church and offered my assistance. The workers were only too happy to have me pitch in. Tables were set up with cups of water for those who were thirsty. There were chairs for those who needed to rest. The church doors were open to anyone who desired prayer, food, or comfort. Many people stopped by asking for prayer or for assistance in locating loved ones.

I helped out the best I could. I talked to people who were crying, upset, confused, afraid for themselves and their families and friends. I offered refreshments, helped them make phone calls, and encouraged them to "hold on" or "just try to make it home." Some people wanted prayer, and I offered prayer for them. Some needed to hear that "God is still in control, no matter what." Somehow, offering these words of comfort brought me comfort, too.

After helping out for several hours, I finally just walked home. There I found all my family, who had also been struggling to make it back. We couldn't give each other enough hugs and kisses—we were so happy that God had spared our lives!

Many thoughts come to mind when I think of September 11. From what I saw of people helping one another, I truly believe it is an invitation to the nation to come together for peace, love, and harmony, even in tragedy. It is also a reminder to turn to God, to prepare ourselves for the day when Jesus will come again, and to avoid putting all our trust in man.

Finally, I will always remember how the Lord spoke to me and gave me peace and guidance. Right in the middle of that very dark situation, I experienced Jesus keeping his promise that he will not forsake us. If I could hear his voice and receive his peace even on September 11, why shouldn't I be optimistic, encouraged, and unafraid as I go about my everyday life?

Praying with a King
By Judy Grivas
Aberdeen, New Jersey

O our God, ... we do not know what to do, but our eyes are on you. (2 Chronicles 20:12)

When I married him in 1967, Phil was a police officer working in one of the most dangerous precincts in New York City. Once, he and his partner were leaving a building with a man in custody when they discovered their patrol car had been set on fire. After that episode, if my husband was late getting home from work, my mind would race with terrible possibilities. But even then God was beginning to teach me to rely on him and not dwell on my fears.

After six years as a police officer, my husband was accepted into the FBI as a special agent. He investigated bank robberies and other major cases. Then he joined the SWAT (Special Weapons and Tactics) team. Sometimes he would leave home at 2:00 a.m. in order to prepare to make an arrest later in the morning. I'd see him out the door with a kiss and a silent prayer. Many nights I'd fall asleep with my rosary in my hands.

Some years later, Phil was made SWAT commander. On his first day as commander, he received an unexpected summons to join other SWAT teams immediately in Atlanta. Prisoners had taken over the federal penitentiary there and were holding guards hostage. He called home, asked me to throw some of his belongings in a bag, stopped by to pick it up, and was in the air the same day.

I prayed more than I ever had before, yet the conflict did not end quickly. As it dragged on, I looked for direction and encouragement in Scripture. One day, I discovered it in the example of a godly Old Testament king. At a time when Judah was threatened by attack and invasion from three different peoples, King Jehoshaphat had voiced a plea to God with which I could relate. Just as I was feeling anxious, fearful, and unable to handle any more waiting, Jehoshaphat must also have felt that way. Yet even in his fear, he prayed.

Standing before the people, he reminded God of his promises to "hear and save" (2 Chronicles 20:9). Not that *God* needed any reminding! It was God's people who needed to recall and affirm God's faithfulness to them in the past. Ultimately pleading "we do not know what to do, but our eyes are on you" (20:12), Jehoshaphat put the entire situation in God's hands. In an act of faith, the king surrendered all to God. How relieved he must have been when God answered that he himself would take care of matters—"for the battle is not yours but God's" (20:15).

I knew I had to do what Jehoshaphat had done. As sincerely and wholeheartedly as I could, I placed my husband and the entire crisis at the penitentiary firmly in God's hands. About two weeks after the hostage situation began, it was resolved. There was one death—a knife-wielding prisoner chasing an unarmed guard was shot by a guard in the tower—but how much worse it might have been.

I had many more occasions to remember Jehoshaphat, and many more invitations to imitate his prayer. Our lives were never predictable. At one point, my husband began to keep a fully packed suitcase in the trunk of his car because he never knew when an unexpected assignment would come up. Often (in the old days before everyone had a cell phone!), he wouldn't even be able to call or send a message to let me know where he was or when he might be home. I learned never to be surprised, and I began to pay close attention to the news so that I could sometimes hazard a guess as to his whereabouts.

Through it all, prayer was my way of dealing with my life. How often I turned my eyes to God when I did not know what to do! How often I asked him to "hear and save"! How often I reminded myself that the battle is God's!

My husband is semi-retired now and although, in some ways, our lives have calmed down considerably, I still find opportunities to make Jehoshaphat's prayer my own. I expect I always will.

The Bookmark
By Jack Butler, Ph.D.
Wichita Falls, Texas

Do not let your hearts be troubled. (John 14:1)

What sorts of things constitute a parent's worst nightmare? Discovering that a child is on drugs or failing in school? Learning that a child has a chronic, life-threatening health problem? Seeing him or her still living at home long beyond the time when they should be independent? Getting that middle-of-the-night phone call with news of some injury, or worse?

I got the phone call. It came as we were heading into a summer that was going to be special for our family. We had two graduation parties planned—one from college and one from medical school—and I was retiring from the Air Force. We were finally out of the college tuition business forever! However, this spirit of celebration came crashing down on June 8, when the phone rang at 1:20 a.m. I answered, expecting bad news about my ninety-year-old mother-in-law. Instead, I heard the voice of the fiancée of our youngest son, Jeremy. She was calling from an emergency room in Savannah, Georgia, to tell us that Jeremy had been shot. A man with a gun had surprised and robbed the two of them as they were returning home after work.

I cannot remember what I said to my wife. I could not function or think clearly. Shock, paralysis—I am not sure how to describe my experience except to say that I felt turned inside out. Of course, we could not sleep. Then about 3:00 a.m., Jeremy called us from his home. His arm was in a sling but he was alive—and even able to joke about needing assistance to go to the bathroom. His sense of humor was intact. As for me, I remained very disturbed, even terrified.

For a long time, I had been in the habit of reciting the prayer on my favorite holy card. Known as St. Teresa of Avila's "bookmark," it was found after her death, written on a piece of paper in her breviary. Reflecting daily on this card had always been an important help in times of stress. It was a way to ponder Jesus' own words, which may have inspired the prayer in the first place: "Do not let your hearts be troubled" (John 14:1).

The prayer goes:

Let nothing disturb you;
Let nothing frighten you.
All things are passing.

God never changes.
Patience obtains all things.
Nothing is wanting to him
Who possesses God.
God alone suffices.

But in the weeks following my son's shooting, it was hard to connect with the ideas on my favorite holy card. For a while, anxiety and worry even sidetracked my daily habit of reading and reflecting on it. "All things are passing...." How would this ever pass? I could not calm down and recover. As one priest said, with traumatic events, "it can take ten minutes to upset someone and ten years to calm them down."

For weeks after the shooting, I had terrible insomnia and kept waking up between 1:00 and 2:00 a.m. Gradually, however, I did get back to meditating on the bookmark, especially the middle part: "God never changes." Its message sank in. Deep down, I know that God never changes, no matter what rain, wind, or lightning may occur in life. It is quieting and comforting to know that we may waver, but God does not.

Reflecting on the holy card also redirected my attention to the things that really matter in life. "Nothing is wanting to him who possesses God. God alone suffices." Any illusion that trying to be a nice, normal Air Force family would somehow confer immunity from tragedy was burst on June 8, 1999. Now, as I seek to put my trust in God, I especially value all that points me to him. A Cursillo lesson taught me that an "isolated Christian is a paralyzed Christian." Knowing that I will fail if I try to go it alone, I am thankful for my antidotes for paralysis—the Church, the sacraments, my daily rosary, Scripture, and *The Word Among Us*.

My son's brush with death has left its mark. My wife and I are no longer entertained by violent movies and television shows. My classic war movie collection remains untouched. Going past any cemetery upsets me even now. I carry the bookmark in my pocket now and reflect on it more than ever. And I have come to see that St. Teresa was right: Patience does obtain all things. All things do pass.

On December 29, 2001, our family celebrated as Jeremy and his fiancée, our town's prima ballerina, were married in our parish. You can guess what one of my wedding gifts was: They each got a copy of my favorite holy card!

When the Shepherd Leads
By Lorrenne Mulherin
Cedar Rapids, Iowa

The LORD is my shepherd,
I shall not want. (Psalm 23:1)

When I was a little girl, the only time I remember hearing the twenty-third psalm was at the funeral of someone I loved. Consequently, it was not my favorite psalm. I was unable to understand that people were comforted by its beautiful words. But a nighttime experience and God's grace have changed my perception.

It was 1:00 a.m. I woke suddenly, terror filling my whole being. I hoped that I was dreaming, but I was not. The terror reflected the reality that confronted me in this awful moment of truth. Many months before, we had been told that my husband, Glen, might die of the cancer he was fighting. Although the experimental treatment was no longer effective and melanoma had invaded both of his lungs, I had not let myself accept the likelihood of his death. Now, with a certainty I could not deny, I knew it was going to happen.

I looked over at my husband. He seemed to be sleeping so peacefully. I could not imagine living without him. We had been "one" for more than forty-five years. He had been there for me—loving, providing, supporting, and encouraging. How could I go on without my other half? I could not bear the thought. I had never experienced such fear.

I bounded from our bed begging God to help me. Never had I needed him more. I almost ran for my Bible. Without even thinking, I turned to Psalm 23, sat down in Glen's chair, and began to read.

The LORD is my shepherd, I shall not want;
he makes me lie down in green pastures.
He leads me beside still waters; he restores my soul.
He leads me in paths of righteousness for his name's sake.
Even though I walk through the valley of the shadow
of death,
I fear no evil; for thou art with me;
Thy rod and thy staff, they comfort me....

I read very slowly, over and over again. I wanted not only to understand—I wanted to *know* the Lord as my Good Shepherd who controls my destiny, who never slumbers or sleeps, who cares and comforts me. This is what happened during the next two hours. Gently, my Shepherd led me through my fears to green pastures and beside still waters. He restored my soul and my peace.

I was so earnestly seeking God in his word that I was oblivious to what he was doing in me. Then I realized that I had been changed, restored. Even though I was still in the valley of the shadow of death, the terror was gone. I had been given the gift of "peace which passes all understanding" (Philippians 4:7). I went back to bed knowing and believing that both Glen and I would be all right, no matter what was going to happen. The terrible fear never came back.

Glen lived only two more months. I was able to remain strong and at peace as my Good Shepherd comforted and led me through the dark valley.

The twenty-third psalm no longer reminds me of death. It is now one of my most loved psalms. It has given me a way of life. I like being a lamb, loved and cared for by the Good Shepherd.

From Grief to Gladness
By Victor Edame
Nigeria

*Those who have died believing in Christ will rise to hope first.
(1 Thessalonians 4:16, Today's English Version)*

I used to grieve so much whenever someone died. I would think about how caring, loving, and friendly that person was. What a loss! If it was the family breadwinner who had died, I mourned because the rest of the family would lose their support. I grieved that none of the dead can return to life to relieve the pain of those they loved and left behind. And whenever a death occurred under especially tragic circumstances—by major accidents, drownings, ritual murder, warfare, fire, earthquake, or epidemic—my grief was even harder to bear. Perhaps you have felt this way, too.

Then, while studying my Bible, I came across this verse: "Those who have died believing in Christ will rise to hope first" (1 Thessalonians 4:16). As I meditated on this, my grief was turned to the unending joy of hope—if I die in Christ, I shall meet again with those who have also died in him! I remembered Jesus' own words: "I am the resurrection and the life. Those who believe in me, even though they die, will live" (John 11:25).

Jesus does not condemn our weeping for the dead. After all, he wept before the tomb of Lazarus (John 11:35). He knows how we feel and cares for us in our sorrow. But because of Christ's resurrection, the story does not end with death and weeping! Rather, when someone dies, we the living should take their death to heart as an inspiration to a closer relationship with God. When the deceased is someone who loved the Lord, we should be consoled that this person lived a worthy life. Through Jesus, whose blood at the cross has reconciled us with God, we can hope to meet them again—never to be parted.

I hope that this verse will help you as much as it has helped me. Think about it, and let God turn your pain to peace, your grief and sorrow to the joy of unending hope in Jesus.

Rest for My Soul
By Magdalene Omo Gunning
Old Karu, Alouja, Nigeria

Come unto me, all ye that labor and are heavy laden, and I will give you rest. (Matthew 11:28, KJV)

When I was a teenager, there was a time when I felt very burdened. My heart was heavy with worries, and there were always family quarrels and bickering that left me distraught. I could not talk to anyone about my problems, and I had not the slightest idea how to tackle the question of getting into a university. My heart indeed knew no peace. Everything was bottled up deep within me.

One day, while walking across the dining room, I noticed the family Bible. It was usually with my mother, but there it lay on the dining table. "Who put this Bible here?" I wondered. Feeling pulled towards it in an irresistible way, I drew close. I remember that the Bible was a King James Version, with the Lord's words printed in red. It was open to the Gospel of St. Matthew. My eyes focused on Matthew 11:28-30:

Come unto me, all ye that labor and are heavy laden, and I will give you rest. Take my yoke upon you and learn of me; for I am meek and lowly in heart; and ye shall find rest unto your souls. For my yoke is easy and my burden is light.

I was shocked beyond words. The passage spoke precisely to my problems. Here was almighty God telling me I should rest my burdened heart in peace in him! I was only too glad to be relieved of my problems. I read the verses once, let their full meaning sink in, and then began reading them a second time.

I had just finished the first sentence—"Come unto me"—when I felt called to place all the hope I could muster in my heart in these living words. They truly were "living." Suddenly my trust and faith awakened, and the good Lord took all my burdens, pains, and worries away.

Yes, when I laid the heaviness in my heart on Jesus' words, they came alive and carried my burden. Instantly, I had such profound peace of mind that I cannot find the words to describe it. I felt free, happy, without any care in the world. How good the Lord is! He is always there for us, almighty and all-powerful to help us in every way. How easy it would be to follow Jesus if we learned to trust and believe in him completely.

A Light in the Darkness
By Nancy Baker
College Station, Texas

Now you don't need to be afraid of the dark any more.
(Psalm 91:5, Living Bible)

Depression draped itself around me like a shroud. Bruised black clouds rolled in from the west, promising an ugly, wet evening. As I hung up the phone in my office at work, tears filled my eyes. They came so easily these days. Ted had been delayed. Instead of being home for dinner, he would arrive late. "Nothing to cry about, Nancy," I whispered aloud. But my spirits sagged, and that familiar defeated feeling climbed on my back again.

I had battled this demon called depression so often in the months since we had moved that I recognized his presence immediately. Sometimes, he came in the form of exhaustion. Other times, he was a not-wanting-to-face-the-world feeling. My ability to take things in stride was nonexistent, and the performance of even simple everyday tasks seemed beyond the realm of possibility.

I was sure there was something wrong with me physically, but my doctor assured me that "demon depression" was a frequent visitor to those going through change. I had moved from the city to the country, leaving my grown children and my long-established friends. I left a lovely brick four-bedroom home and took up residence in a tiny unfinished cabin. I accepted a new job, after twelve years at my old one.

Rain pelted down as I settled in for the twenty-five-mile drive home from work. Self-pity seated herself beside me. She told me how cold the cabin would be—how muddy and bumpy the country road was, how treacherous in this kind of weather. She reminded me of the loneliness at the cabin and how eerie it would seem during a thunderstorm.

At the cabin, safe and semi-dry, I determined to make use of a weapon I had learned about to combat depression. "Keep busy," I said aloud. Carrying a hot cup of tea upstairs, I snuggled down in bed with my photo album. Placing the pictures in the album brought back good memories. I smiled in spite of myself and felt my depression lift a bit. I glanced at the clock radio beside my bed. Eight o'clock! Ted would be home soon.

Suddenly there came an explosion of thunder so loud that I not only heard but felt it inside me—it seemed to be right there in my bedroom. Then all fell silent, except for the patter of rain on the roof. The cabin was plunged into a darkness even more enveloping than my depression. Was that the odor of something burning? All my senses were being bombarded simultaneously. Fear began as a hard knot in the pit of my stomach and spread rapidly to my trembling hands and legs. The terror nearly paralyzed me.

Flashes of lightning lit up the room crazily, but not sufficiently for me to determine what had happened. Feeling my way down the stairs, I found the flashlight, candles, and matches. Investigation revealed my clock radio in pieces. I later learned that lightning had struck a nearby transformer, sending a surge of electricity that caused the clock radio to explode.

I was badly shaken and worried about Ted. It was now well past the time when he had said he would be home. Fully alert to the storm's fury, I sat in the dark, with lightning flashing, candles flickering, and thunder booming. I grew more and more agitated and jumped at every unexpected noise. My imagination ran rampant when I thought about Ted. The vision of his being swept off the road was vivid and clear.

I knew I should pray, but words wouldn't come. Triggered by my fright and anxiety for Ted, the weight of the weeks of depression crashed in on me. Tears flowed down my cheeks, slowly at first, then faster and faster; they tumbled over each other until, like the rain outside, they fell in a torrent. "Lord, help me," I sobbed. Immediately, my mind filled with the thought, *Read my word.* I recognized the Lord's prodding. Often in the past, when I wanted to pray but couldn't find the words, I had come across an appropriate Scripture. When praying for someone, I learned to personalize my prayer by inserting the person's name into the passage. I was amazed at how often Scripture spoke the perfect words for a situation.

What to read? I knew the psalms to be soothing and comforting. Randomly, I flipped to the ninety-first psalm. Astonishment filled me, and I sucked in my breath quickly. The first sentence the rays of my unsteady flashlight picked up was, "Now you don't need to be afraid of the dark any more" (Psalm 91:5). Tears of gratitude replaced tears of fear. The Lord was with me.

Feeling comforted, I eagerly read the whole psalm and discovered that, with some adapting, I could also use it as a prayer for Ted's safety: "This I declare, that he alone is Ted's refuge, his place of safety... For he rescues Ted from every trap and protects him... He will shield Ted with his wings!... His faithful promises are Ted's armor.... For he orders his angels to protect Ted wherever he goes."

As I continued to read and reread Psalm 91, peace entered my weary soul. At last, I laid down my burdens. I no longer wore the burial garment of depression. And my prayers were answered within the hour, when Ted trudged in, exhausted but unharmed.

My Two Joshuas
By Jane T. Leischer
Medford, Wisconsin

Have I not told you: Be strong and stand firm? Be fearless then, be confident, for go where you will, Yahweh your God is with you. (Joshua 1:9, Jerusalem Bible)

On July 24, 1998, Joshua, our first grandchild, entered our lives. His birth came as I was recovering from colon surgery following a diagnosis of cancer. Since my husband Tom and I wanted to drive to Cleveland to spend a few days with Joshua, I obtained the oncologist's okay to put off chemotherapy for two weeks. She probably suspected that holding and cuddling my grandson would facilitate the healing process.

I returned home with renewed courage to face my treatment—three eight-week cycles of continuous drip chemotherapy from an infusion pump that would be surgically implanted into my chest wall. On August 3, the day when my "buddy" was to be implanted, Joshua came back into my life in a different way. This time it was the Old Testament Book of Joshua that I encountered. As I searched Scripture during my early morning prayer time, Joshua 1:9 gave me what I needed. Yes! God was with me, therefore I could "be strong and stand firm." I could face the day "fearless" and "confident." It surely was not my strength that got me through the doors of ambulatory surgery that day.

From then on, every Monday was a special day for holding onto those words, "be fearless," as the nurse removed the needle and tubing from the pump part and prepared me for a refill and another week's round of chemotherapy. The weeks passed, and I continued clinging to Joshua 1:9. Finally, though, the side effects became more than I could bear. On a sunny Sunday afternoon, just a few days short of completing the last cycle of treatment, my chemotherapy was ended.

Now came a different fear. Did I have enough faith to let go of chemotherapy? Could I trust God with the outcome?

My tests came back normal. Blood levels continue to be normal. I'm on a different journey now. The possibility of recurrence is always in the background, but I have lived cancer free for five years. As I thank God for bringing me healing, I continue to "stand firm" in the confidence that, go where I will, my God is with me.

10

A Better Way

At first glance, you might find the stories in this chapter a somewhat eclectic collection.

A widow reconsiders her decision to remarry. A military spouse reflects on the place of humor in the Christian life and adjusts her approach accordingly. A prison inmate is led to read a gospel passage in a different way. A Good Samaritan-type learns to stop being a pushover. Two people give up resentment: One gets a new lease on life; the other finds help for a tedious task.

The connecting thread that links these varied stories could be described as "a change of direction." Essentially, that's what conversion is. Deciding to follow Jesus means leaving the broad, well-traveled road and walking the narrow road that leads to life. But conversion isn't a one-time event! Every day, in important areas of our lives and in small ones, we're invited to choose God's way over our own. Often this involves saying no to sin. Sometimes, however, the Holy Spirit is revealing an alternative we hadn't thought of—a "better way" that can bring us and others more life and joy.

As you read these stories, remember that you are loved by a God who has a more wonderful plan for you—both in this life and in the next—than you can begin to imagine. Ask the Holy

Spirit to stretch your mind so that you can see where he is inviting you to reject sin or simply to choose a better way.

Think About It!

"We are never completely converted," wrote the Brazilian archbishop and spiritual writer Dom Helder Camara. "We have to keep on converting ourselves every day.... Conversion ought to be going on every day, since self-centeredness is ever-living. They say it only dies a few hours after we ourselves are dead."

Pray It!

Take a few moments to reflect on God's love for you. Let his love draw you to an increased desire for him and his ways. Here are two Scripture passages to help you as you speak to the Lord about these things—very simply, from the heart:

For surely I know the plans I have for you, says the LORD, plans for your welfare and not for harm, to give you a future with hope. Then when you call upon me and come and pray to me, I will hear you. When you search for me, you will find me. (Jeremiah 29:11-13)

Do not be conformed to this world, but be transformed by the renewing of your minds, so that you may discern what is the will of God—what is good and acceptable and perfect. (Romans 12:2)

Just Say No!
By Vicky Galczynski
Jarrettsville, Maryland

And he sighed deeply in his spirit and said, "Why does this generation ask for a sign? Truly I tell you, no sign will be given to this generation." (Mark 8:12)

"Just say no." The familiar statement to deter kids from using drugs has become my husband's battle cry. He adopted it soon after our wedding, when he realized I was one of those smiling, pushover people who couldn't say no to an ice cream salesman at the North Pole.

My tendency developed when I was a child and took to heart the Franciscan sisters' instruction to be the Good Samaritan, to help those in need, and to lend an understanding ear. Now as an adult, I find it hard to deny anyone any request.

At church on Sunday, when the priest or deacon begins his emphatic request for more casseroles for the needy or help with the next spaghetti supper, I hear my name at the beginning and end of each statement. When a "works of mercy" team is in the vestibule signing people up for their next event, I feel their eyes desperately requesting my assistance. When the phone rings and it's a good cause—whether it's to volunteer at my son's school or to stuff envelopes for a mailing—I usually say yes, even if I have to fit it in by writing sideways on my full calendar. Feeling it's my duty, I rarely fail to offer assistance, no matter what the cost to myself or my family. Considering I have a number of health problems, the cost can be quite high. Still I think to myself, "But Jesus did so much for others, didn't he? God has given me so much. I can't refuse to give back, can I?"

I prayed that God would tell me when to offer assistance and when to "just say no," but I had difficulty hearing his answers until I started looking to the example of Jesus himself.

I sifted through the gospels until, one day, I found it: Jesus *did* say no. It happened when he was confronted with a demand from some of the scribes and Pharisees who were "seeking a sign from heaven" (Mark 8:11-12; Matthew 12:38-42; 16:1-4). Whether they intended to trip him up or really thought they needed to see even more proofs of his power, Jesus refused. Enough was enough.

Jesus could easily have worked just one more "sign" or miracle, I'm sure. And it wasn't because he didn't care that he said no. Quite simply, he knew he had done enough. Now it was time for others to do their part. For the scribes and Pharisees, that meant acting on what they had already seen Jesus do by recognizing him as Messiah and putting their faith in him.

Here was my answer! Sometimes things that need doing are best left to others. In fact, trying to do and be everything for other people is unfair to them as well as to me. It may be robbing them of the opportunity to grow and to explore their faith. In a sense, it may even be denying God. Isn't this what happens when we try to undertake every task on our own, as if we and not God were ultimately responsible for overseeing everything?

Now that I know there is a time to say yes and a time to say no, I'm a little slower at committing myself. And although I can't eliminate all spur-of-the-moment requests, I do tend to consider them more carefully. I take a little time to sit down with a picture of Jesus and my calendar and ask, "Are my actions best for me? For my family? For others?" And sometimes I do say no.

Laughing All the Way
By Juliana Jones
Springfield, Virginia

Strength and dignity are her clothing,
and she laughs at the time to come. (Proverbs 31:25)

Let's face it: laughter and humor are not spoken of a great deal in the Bible. When the word "laughter" is used, it usually points unfavorably to the fool, the drunkard, or the unbeliever. Take Sirach 21:20, for example: "A fool raises his voice when he laughs, but the wise smile quietly." I find this somewhat disheartening, since I do a lot of smiling and giggling, with an occasional belly laugh—and still consider myself sensible. Should I feel embarrassed that I am enjoying myself, perhaps too loudly for some? No, I think it's my way of spreading God's love around. My laughter is used to heal.

Recently, the Holy Spirit led me to a passage that has helped me reflect on laughter and the good uses to which it can be put. It comes from the description of a capable wife that is in Proverbs, one of my favorite books: "Strength and dignity are her clothing, and she laughs at the time to come" (Proverbs 31:25). To me this means being confidently and joyfully ready to face the struggles ahead without trepidation, secure in God's embrace.

As a military spouse, I can use some of that worry-free optimism in facing the sobering realities of the world situation and my husband's job. Then there are the common challenges of frequent uprooting. Not long ago, we were facing yet another move—this one from Alaska to Virginia, our seventh in twenty years of marriage. What does it take to get us through the initial shock of a transfer? Humor helps in a huge way, I've discovered. Without acting overly silly, I can set an upbeat, "laughing at the future" mood. Three teenage sons with endless appetites, a dog with bladder problems, and a temperamental vehicle—the raw material for a hilarious and healing journey is there, if I choose to see it that way.

And so I told myself as we traveled cross country, I won't worry if the transmission goes out on the van again, or if we run out of water driving through a dry part of the country, or if the dog gets carsick. No problem! I will be filled with the Holy Spirit, ready to do his will and pass the joy around, as well as the paper towels. I know that God is by my side to guide me, give me strength along the way, and hold my hand through whatever trial I might face.

And surely this joyful, apprehension-free attitude will see me through my teens' dating years! It will also see me through the days when I've been volunteered to chaperone a field trip, but don't get told about it until that morning. Despite the stress, I am clothed in the strength of the Lord. Because of his presence in me, I am able to maintain my cheerfulness and fortitude to face what is just around the bend in the road.

I've come to see that this "laughter at the days to come" doesn't mean snickering bitterly at the world. I should not use sarcasm as a cover for ridiculing my neighbor or for being irreverent. This is an improper use of the gift of humor because it brings division instead of unity. But if I use my humor as a gift, a grace handed to me by God to continue his work, it is perfectly appropriate.

The dispersal of the good news through laughter, harmless jokes, and lots of fun is my vocation. If the Holy Spirit moves me to perform slapstick along with my storytelling, I oblige. Who can live without laughter, a nudge from a friend whose joy is infectious? Shouldn't we share this happiness we've found in Christ? Laughter is contagious and can uplift spirits both in times of distress and in the humdrum monotony of daily living. It is therefore my pleasure to help people with their adventure here on earth, encouraging them to find their delight in worry-free living and a God-filled life.

Drawing on both Sirach 21:20 and Proverbs 31:25, I've come to the conclusion that I must live each day filled with the grace of glee that God has bestowed upon me. I must also balance it with dignity and poise, maintaining a sense of decorum that points to a wise and graceful person. With this attitude I can help not only my family and myself, but I can also do as Jesus did and help others in the community to find peace within their hearts. Every day I can step out into the world with a kind smile on my lips and laughter in my heart—all to share the love I've found in Jesus Christ our Savior.

Love and Forgiveness
By Donna Serna-Lopez
Denver, Colorado

Whenever you stand praying, forgive. (Mark 11:25)

Nearly four years ago, I began studying Scripture at the Catholic Biblical School in Denver. I had no idea what God had in store for me. I just knew that I was at a crossroads in my life. I was searching—for what, I didn't even know. I was tired and burnt out; there was this void in my life. I had been in the nursing field for thirty years. I had worked in hospitals, nursing homes, community health, clinics—you name it. Now, employed at a large local hospital, I was feeling unhappy. My attitude was: "I have no more to give, and please don't ask." I felt guilty for having these feelings. I began to pray, asking God to show me the way.

As I studied the Scriptures, I entered into the period that I now think of as my desert search. Something very important began to happen to me in the area of forgiveness.

Having experienced some painful situations growing up, I had struggled with forgiveness for years. I thought I had worked things through, but there was still this piece of baggage that I carried around and that often made me feel sorry for myself. It was resentment toward my mother. I had always felt that I could never please her; no matter how hard I tried, it never seemed to be good enough.

One day, a long-suffering friend who had listened time and again as I shared my feelings said to me, "Donna, have you ever thought that maybe your mother did the best she could?" For some reason, this simple statement stopped me in my tracks. I realized that my friend was exactly right. Suddenly I saw my mother in a whole different light—as a woman who was and still is feisty, wise without the benefit of a formal education. The daughter of a migrant farmer, she grew up during the Great Depression, working in the fields from the time she could walk. She knew the meaning of hard labor. She had never found it easy to be affectionate or to praise her children, but she *had* done the best she could. With this realization, I felt an inner peace. I let go and forgave her.

In my study of the Scriptures, I had often reflected on Jesus' call to forgiveness: "Whenever you stand praying, forgive, if you have anything against anyone; so that your Father in heaven may also forgive you your trespasses" (Mark 11:25). Once I stopped harboring resentment, I opened myself to true forgiveness and its benefits for my own life. I could relate to what Father Benedict J. Groeschel describes in his wonderful book, *The Journey Toward God*:

Every person who ever meditated on the Lord's Prayer knows that forgiveness is a very special Christian obligation.

And so we struggle to forgive, but often reach only the desire to forgive, without real forgiveness. This desire and the attempts that forgiveness inspires are good acts in themselves, but they are not the fullness of charity.... The person illuminated by the irresistible and unquestioned presence of God knows in fact that he has nothing to lose. Then forgiveness flows along with mercy, understanding, and magnanimity, or boundless generosity. Not only can the person say, "It is no longer I who live, but Christ who lives in me" (Galatians 2:20); he can also say, "It is no longer I who forgive, but Christ who forgives in me."

Peace and love are the gifts that forgiveness has given me. Before I could truly love, I had to learn how to forgive. I realized that not only was I being too hard on everyone else but on myself as well. I learned to forgive myself. I began to see people in a whole different light. Now I find that I am no longer so quick to become angry. My job no longer seems like a burden.

I still have so much to learn in my study of the Scriptures. I feel like I've only skimmed the surface. My four-year course of study is at an end. I will be graduating from the Biblical school soon. Will I remember to listen to God speaking to me in a tiny whisper? Will I have the courage to speak against injustices in the world, or will I hide under a bushel? My God has blessed me. I hope that I can be a blessing to others!

Repentance in the Rain
By James Birong
Carrollton, Ohio

See to it ... that no root of bitterness springs up and causes trouble. (Hebrews 12:15)

The sky was gray and overcast—not the most promising weather for the job I had to do. But the pine tree seedlings behind my dental office needed to be mowed, and this was Saturday, the only day of the week when I had time to do it. "Gee, Lord," I prayed, "it looks an awful lot like rain. Please hold off the rain for the next five hours." Then I fought with myself, thinking that this was kind of a petty request. I felt selfish, too. After all, the farmer over the hill was probably praying for rain!

Finally, I revised my prayer and told the Lord that I wanted his will, and not mine. "*You're* in control here. If the farmer needs the rain more than I need to mow, then let it rain. But if you can see clear to hold it off for the next five hours, I thank you ahead of time."

As I surrendered the situation to the Lord, I felt real peace and joy come over me. Wow! I just *knew* he would hold off that rain. I began to sing alleluias, praising him with all my heart. I was filled with joy and wonder at God's graciousness and mercy. I sang his praises for a good half hour: "Rejoice in the Lord always.... In everything by prayer and supplication with thanksgiving let your requests be made known to God. And the peace of God, which surpasses all understanding, will guard your hearts and your minds in Christ Jesus" (Philippians 4:4, 6-7). Then I fell into the boredom of mowing row after row.

About three hours later, when I was more than halfway up the field, I was jolted to attention by a big drop of rain hitting me in the face. Another drop landed on the muffler, then another on the hood. I looked up, startled. The sky was black, and the rain was coming. I was about to get soaked. Thinking back to my prayer, I said, "What happened, Lord? You promised!"

I remembered, then, what I had been thinking about once my prayers of praise had given way to the monotony of mowing. I had been getting bitter and resentful toward my partner in the dental practice. *Why isn't he out here mowing instead of me? I'm the one who fixed the holes in the driveway. He hasn't done anything.* I had really been hateful.

I looked up and said, "Sorry, Lord," as the rain hit my face. "I shouldn't have been resentful. My partner does many things that I can't, and this mowing is one thing I can do. He's got arthritis, so shoveling the gravel in the driveway should be my job. I'm sorry for this bitterness." As I finished this thought, the rain began to fade. By the end of the next row, it had stopped. I mowed two more hours under terribly threatening skies, but there was not one more drop of rain.

I began to sing God's praises again, with an additional prayer: "Lord, remind me every day that I must keep on loving—my patients, my employees, my partner, my kids, my wife. I must never let the evil one trick me into resentment and bitterness. Then I'll truly be your disciple."

God Is My King

By Mary E. Killmond
Woodland Hills, California

Then all the elders of Israel gathered together and came to Samuel ... and said to him ... "Appoint for us, then, a king to govern us, like other nations." (1 Samuel 8:4-5)

"I love you, Jesus, my love. Grant that I may love you always, and then do with me as you will." This prayer of St. Alphonsus Liguori comes up unbidden in me in times of crisis and joy. It came up very often in the days, weeks, and months following my husband's death from melanoma at the age of fifty-eight. The disease progressed very rapidly, and he died only five days after being hospitalized.

We had been in the middle of our lives, finally getting the hang of really enjoying and appreciating our large and maturing family and each other's very different personalities. I had not yet turned fifty. Five of our eight children were still at home; our youngest child was only eight. My husband's acting career, his first love, had once been unpredictable but had held steady over the past five years. I was teaching in a local Catholic school. We also owned a Catholic book and gift shop. Then suddenly there was no more "we." My husband was gone, and I was left to continue raising our children, find my way through the labyrinth of our finances, and establish new boundaries and borders in our family life.

The days and weeks that followed highlighted every fault and strain in the personality and character of each individual family member and of the family as a whole. We received help from friends that was absolutely life-saving. Even so, our problems were bigger than we could manage. With the help of a grief counselor, we began the painful and difficult work of reconstituting ourselves as a family without a husband and father. There were so many tears. The hurts of the past had to be laid to rest before we could find out how to be this new entity. "This isn't how it was supposed to be!" each of us shouted in our own way. Yet this is how it was. We struggled with so many issues—college, money, discipline, chores, friendships. Every area of life seemed to present some difficulty. Even the family diet was an issue. Two of the girls were vegetarians, two were on low-fat diets, and it was impossible to prepare a family meal without stress and strain.

Somehow we survived and began to heal. Three years were consumed by this process of grieving. Then we began to come back to life. We had a greater respect for one another and a reborn sense of hope.

I began to feel freer than I had in years and realized that I was interested in life again. I was attending a religious conference when I recognized that I wanted to feel like a woman once more. Looking around the crowded room, I said to my friend, "I feel like shouting, 'Here I am, and I'm available!'"

It was there that I ran into a man I had met many years ago at the same conference. His wife had died more than a year before. We talked about the possibility of getting together, and he asked for my phone number. It was really rather exciting. He was energetic, good-looking, and seemed about my age. I thought to myself, "We'll see!"

When he called to ask me out on a date not long thereafter, I felt ready to begin this part of my life again. What followed was a delightful, exciting, happy round of outings and stay-at-homes. We went for long drives, discovering and sharing places that we had never been before and places we had each loved in the past. We discovered we had so much in common and so many shared interests. There was a wonderful chemistry between us that heightened the enjoyment of every discovery and shared event. He said to me on one occasion, "When you've lost a spouse it's impossible to look forward to celebrating a golden wedding anniversary, but it is possible to look forward to a second twenty-fifth." We began to talk about marriage. We were thrilled with each other and with this possible new opportunity at life. It seemed to be a gift from God.

I was so thrilled that I did not pay serious attention to the fact that there were some red flags. There was the disagreement with my daughter, which he handled so poorly that there was continuing unease between them. There was the rudeness to my best friend over a conversation topic that came up when she and her husband made a foursome with us. There was the impatience with my normal routines, leading to requests like, "Couldn't you please take care of that after I leave?" There was the genuine anger at my youngest child over a board game.

The clouds of doubt began to gather. Was this really a "good" match? Was this relationship simply a wonderful excitement, or was it a gift from God? With a heavy heart, I began to pray in earnest and repeatedly took this question to my morning prayer time. I sought God's direction, especially through an approach to Scripture I had used before. It involves pouring out one's heart in prayer and then seeking God's response by opening Scripture several times in faith that it is truly God's living word. Reflecting on the passages that are brought to one's attention in this way can be fruitful over time. The guidance that God is giving often becomes clearer and clearer, as if a fog is lifting.

Several times as I turned to Scripture, a passage came up that I did not connect with at first. It was 1 Samuel 8:1-21, in which the people of Israel tell Samuel that they want to be governed by a king, "like other nations." God had chosen Samuel as a judge to guide the people, but they demand a king who will fight their battles for them. (Was I, like the ungrateful Israelites, looking for someone to fight my battles for me?) Samuel responds with anger, but as he prays, God assures him that the people "have not rejected you, but they have rejected me from being king over them" (1 Samuel 8:7). (Was I, too, rejecting God's kingship?)

God tells Samuel to grant the peoples' request, but also to warn them that the king will make heavy demands. If they persist, they will lose all that is dear to them—their sons and daughters will be pressed into the king's service, and he will have his pick of their crops, flocks, and other goods. The people insist, and the dire predictions are realized.

This warning must have affected me deeply. One night when this man I had come to love made a demand that was clearly out of bounds, I was able to calmly and clearly say, "No." He warned me that if he left, he would not be back. I was able to let him go. He did come back, but as time went on, the rift that had sprung from my "no" and his angry exit widened. Though this was a deeply sad, disappointing loss, I have no regrets. I was not about to give up the beautiful, graced life I and my family had been given. God reigns in our family.

Since then, God has continued to bless us in many ways. I have completed a masters degree in religious studies. Among them, the children have finished three undergraduate and three graduate degrees and have given me seven delightful grandchildren.

As I look back, I praise God that I was able to heed the warning I was given. God is my King, and I am God's humble lady who still prays, "I love you, Jesus, my love. Grant that I may love you always, and then do with me as you will."

Solitude on the Beach
By Lorrenne Mulherin
Cedar Rapids, Iowa

Who then is this, that he commands even the winds and the water, and they obey him? (Luke 8:25)

We had just arrived at our hotel in St. Petersburg, Florida. Opening the door to our balcony, I walked out and couldn't believe what I saw and heard. What a different world from the Iowa farm we had left behind! The white sand beach, the forlorn cry of the seagulls, and the majestic sound of the surf took my breath away. My husband Glen was equally impressed—it was his first exposure to a real ocean beach too.

We took our first beach walk that night and fell in love again. In the days that followed, we walked many oceanside miles together—hand in hand or simply side by side, talking or laughing, sometimes quiet, often experiencing a certain solitude even in the midst of a crowd of walkers. I learned to love that solitude on the beach.

On one particularly nice day, I was walking the beach by myself and sat down on a jetty. As I listened to the surf, I began thinking of the power that was in it. How loud it sounded, even on this calm, lovely day. I tried to envision what it must be like when there was a hurricane and waves were crashing on the shore. I was deeply involved in my thoughts, when, in a way I can't adequately explain, I heard these words: "There is more power in you than in that body of water, because I live in you and I calm the storms." I knew the words came from within myself but were not my own. And they were too clearly spoken to be passed off as my imagination. Somehow, I just knew that Jesus was the one who had spoken to me.

Besides, who but Jesus could calm a storm? I remembered vividly the story of how a terrible gale came up when Jesus was in a boat with his disciples. They were so frightened! Jesus simply gave a command: "He rebuked the wind and the raging waves; they ceased, and there was a calm" (Luke 8:24). I had always believed in Jesus' power, but the words I had just heard brought it home to me in a new way. I felt like shouting, "Yes, I believe! I never really understood before, but I do now!"

The same power and might that could calm a hurricane was at work in me. If I really believed this truth, I realized, it would change me. Indeed, the change began right then and there. I felt tall and strong as I walked back to the hotel—not because of the power of my five-foot-one body, but because of the power of the One who lives in me.

I can say truthfully that I have never been the same since. Lack of confidence, fear, and timidity vanished on the beach that day. What replaced them was a "knowing" of God's presence and power. I now have the faith to believe that I—one person—can make a difference in the world and that there is no limit to what God can do through me if I let him.

A New Way to Approach Scripture
By Mark Sandore
Sonyea, New York

And the people stood by, watching.... (Luke 23:35)

Some time ago, the Catholic chaplain of the correctional facility where I live began to offer a catechesis class in which residents, volunteers, and chaplains gather to discuss, among other things, what it is that makes our faith special. We also share ideas and discuss the readings from the previous Sunday's Mass, particularly the gospel. As we read and reflected on these passages, I found myself becoming more aware of all the varied responses to Jesus in each story.

One Scripture passage that impressed me deeply is from the Gospel of Luke (23:35-43), which describes the crucifixion of Jesus. So many different personalities and elements, and so many connections that speak to me about my own behavior and way of life!

This bit of Scripture intrigued me because it invited me to put myself in the place of the various people who appear in it—but not mainly the admirable ones! It's natural to want to identify with the people who welcomed and received Jesus or who came to him for healing. In Luke 23, however, there are many who did just the opposite. With one exception, these are the characters in whom I recognized something of myself:

"And the *people* stood by, watching" (verse 35). How many times have I been unwilling to get involved out of fear of responsibility or of what others might think?

"The *leaders* scoffed at him" (verse 35). So many times, my arrogance and doubt have kept me apart from the Lord.

"The *soldiers* also mocked him, coming up and offering him sour wine" (verse 36). How many times a day do I offer my Lord my half-hearted attempts to root out my sin, and then judge others for their sins?

"One of the *criminals* who were hanged there kept deriding him" (verse 39). How often have I shown a lack of respect for my Lord and the love he offers me?

"But the *other [criminal]* rebuked him, saying… 'Jesus, remember me when you come into your kingdom'" (verses 40, 42). And how many times have I done what is wrong or failed to do what is right—and yet my Lord is right there to offer me his forgiveness and shower me with his grace?

11

The Gift of Gratitude

What are you grateful for? The men and women who wrote the stories in this chapter mention a wide range of reasons for gratitude—among them salvation, renewal, health, and even *ill* health! As the *Catechism of the Catholic Church* tells us: "Every joy and suffering, every event and need can become the matter for thanksgiving which, sharing in that of Christ, should fill one's whole life" (2648).

So where do you fall on the gratitude scale? Do you remember to thank God for small blessings, or do you tend to accept them unthinkingly? Do major joys move you to readily acknowledge their Giver? What about trials big and small? Would joyful thanks come more easily if you had absolute trust that "all things work together for good for those who love God" (Romans 8:28)?

Think About It!

This good advice comes from St. Frances Cabrini, who cheerfully overcame many trials in order to minister to the needs of Italian immigrants in the United States:

Know that gratitude for God's benefits is one of the riches of the soul, and that ingratitude dries up the fountain of divine graces. Give your tribute of gratitude often to the most loving Jesus. Often look back over your lives and consider the graces that you have received.... God has worked many wonders for you because he loves you well. But remember that all he has done for you up to now is but a slight pledge of his great love. (*The Travels of Mother Frances Xavier Cabrini*)

Pray It!

Reflect on the Scripture verses below, inviting the Holy Spirit to deepen your understanding and knowledge of God's great goodness. As love and gratitude well up in your heart, ask yourself: "How can I thank the Lord for all his goodness to me?"

Rejoice always, pray without ceasing, give thanks in all circumstances; for this is the will of God in Christ Jesus for you. (1 Thessalonians 5:16-18)

I will give thanks to the LORD with my whole heart;
I will tell of all your wonderful deeds.
I will be glad and exult in you;
I will sing praise to your name, O Most High.
(Psalm 9:1-2)

The Best Medicine
By Evelyn Richter
Center Point, Texas

A merry heart doeth good like a medicine.
(Proverbs 17:22, KJV)

It was the Fourth of July weekend. I was in the intensive care unit of our local hospital with a severe case of ureic poisoning due to a blocked kidney stone.

The doctors had given me their prognosis. If they operated to remove the stone, I could die; if they *didn't* operate, I could die—"but let's give it a couple more days and see if it will pass on its own." In the meantime, they started me on antibiotics and went ahead with their weekend holiday plans, leaving instructions with the attending nurses that I should be kept heavily sedated.

In several of my more lucid moments, a nurse wearing the name tag "Anna" would come into my room and check on me. Always when she came in, she was smiling or humming a tune, and she spoke kind words in a most uplifting tone of voice. During one of those visits, I groggily asked her, "Anna, how can you be so cheerful, working with all of us old sick people all the time?"

She gently laid her hand on mine, looked kindly into my eyes, and softly told me her story:

Some years ago, I too was very ill, with no real hope for recovery, as far as the doctors could determine. During his daily visit, the hospital chaplain read the seventeenth chapter of Proverbs to me. When he came to the twenty-second verse, he looked at me and said, "Anna, keep this verse in your heart and mind: 'A merry heart doeth good like a medicine.'"

A merry heart? Under the circumstances, it made no sense. But the chaplain was so sincere when he told me to concentrate on the verse that, sick as I was, I decided to give it a try. I made a conscious effort to think of all the good things God had brought into my life—all of the fun times, the wonderful people. I even sang some songs. I tried to remember funny stories. And you know what? Within a week I was released from the hospital. The doctors called it a miracle. I did, too. I have tried to maintain that merry, happy heart ever since.

With that, Anna left to tend to her other patients—and left me wondering if *I* could do as she had. I didn't think it would be easy. Did God ever promise us an easy road, though? No, but he *did* promise to be with us each step of the way.

So I tried to follow Anna's example. I thought of all the good God had done for me. I remembered his gifts: his precious Son, salvation, eternal life; good family and friends, neighbors, coworkers, and caregivers; help with my material needs ... and so very many gifts that it will take eternity to count them all. Once I started thinking of all the good God does for us, I couldn't help but be merry! And I discovered that the "merry heart" does indeed work like a medicine that furthers the healing process in every area.

But do you know what else God gave me that day, along with the inspiring testimony of my caring nurse, Anna? This is the absolute truth: God gave me a vision of Christ. There in my hospital room, as I was praying and trying to sing my favorite hymn, "Amazing Grace," a sort of white cloud appeared on the wall opposite me. In it I saw the face of Jesus smiling at me. A sudden and immediate peace filled my heart, mind, soul, and body. Within two hours, the kidney stone had passed.

I have had many hospital visits since then, for a variety of problems: complications from rheumatoid arthritis; appendectomy;

removal of three blood clots, my gall bladder, and cataracts; skin cancer surgery; treatment for a variety of broken bones; and more. Through it all, I have tried to keep my heart merry. I have recovered from all of these difficulties, and I share Proverbs 17:22 with everyone I can.

With God Nothing Is Impossible
By Roy Galvan
Beeville, Texas

I do not claim that I have already succeeded or have already become perfect. I keep striving to win the prize for which Christ Jesus has already won me to himself. Of course my friends, I really do not think that I have already won it; the one thing I do, however, is to forget what is behind me and do my best to reach what is ahead. So I run straight toward the goal in order to win the prize, which is God's call through Christ Jesus to the life above. (Philippians 3:12-14, Today's English Version)

When a dark cloud shadows his life and darkens his future, a man has to swallow his pride and accept that he has a problem. By admitting his shortcomings and coming to terms with his problems, he can begin to disperse those dark clouds and allow the light to once again enter his life.

I had such a problem, but in 1985 my life dramatically changed. I got down on my knees and prayed, putting my faith in God and asking Jesus to help me overcome my drug and alcohol addiction. Suddenly, my cravings were gone. The pull of my addiction had disappeared. Soon my feelings of loneliness and the emptiness within me began to fade. I discovered that Jesus was what had been missing from my life.

The years that followed were rough going. I struggled with life's adversities, but as a Christian I continued to walk in the light of the Holy Spirit. Learning more about myself, my family, and everything around me, I started to live and enjoy life with a peace that I never before knew existed.

My spiritual life was blossoming, but still I was struggling to provide for my family. Since I had been out of work for quite some time, money for necessities, bills, and food was becoming more and more scarce. My work at an oil field came to a dead-end. I was forced to find odd jobs, collect aluminum cans, and mow yards for next to nothing. But the Lord had plans for me, and I got a job at the local school district for $3.75 an hour as a janitor. This was truly a blessing for us, as I had been out of steady work for close to a year.

Still, it was very difficult for us to keep our heads above water financially. For nearly three years, my wife would use our only car to take our children to school, while I used her bike for transportation. Finally, in 1988, we were able to purchase a second vehicle for $750, and I began to contract with some real estate companies to do yard work. The work was grueling, but I kept my faith and built my confidence in God.

In 1989 my youngest son graduated from high school and immediately joined the Navy. We were heartsick. The empty house echoed loneliness, and we wandered about in it aimlessly. It was then that we decided to pick ourselves up and go to college. What a challenge it was to work two jobs, further my education, and continue my ministering at the jail and prison! Thank God for my wonderful wife!

I knew God was looking over my shoulder as I excelled in my work, ascending from a janitor to a labor foreman, an electrician, and then on to become director of the department. And it was surely the Lord who helped me pursue his plans to continue my education. It wasn't easy. One major hurdle was that the university is located eighty miles from our hometown. For seven years, I made the twice-a-week journey to class after work to earn my bachelor's degree in human resources.

Seventeen years of sobriety, seventeen years of putting my faith in God—and finally, on August 11, 2000, I received my diploma from Texas A&M University at Kingsville. As I walked toward the stage, looking across the crowd at my wonderful wife and family, it was hard to hold back my tears of joy. All the long days, months, and years of hardship, traveling, and studying had culminated in this wonderful moment.

Many times since 1985, I had drawn hope and encouragement from Philippians 3, verses 12-14. I continue to do so, for the greatest prize is still ahead. And so, "I do not claim that I have already succeeded or have already become perfect. I keep striving to win the prize for which Christ Jesus has already won me to himself." I thank God every day for being at my side and for all the blessings that he has bestowed upon my family. And I press on, doing my best to "run straight toward the goal in order to win the prize, which is God's call through Christ Jesus to the life above."

A Questionable Gift
By Vicky Galczynski
Jarrettsville, Maryland

In my flesh I complete what is lacking in Christ's afflictions for the sake of his body, that is, the church. (Colossians 1:24)

Have you ever been given a gift that seemed at first like more trouble than it was worth—something you considered too trendy (that first microwave oven), too difficult to learn (the newest computer software), or too hard to fit into your way of doing things (replacing the disposable razor with the newest electric model)? But then have you ever discovered that such a gift, if given a chance, really did make things easier or brighter or caused you to look at life in a whole new way?

I've been blessed with such a gift. It came sixteen years ago, without wrapping or bows, and was definitely of the "some assembly required" variety. It made its first appearances in numerous physical symptoms like frequent headaches, muscle weakness, and vision loss. They presented themselves as puzzle pieces to the myriad of physicians who examined me, but finally I was diagnosed with multiple sclerosis.

In my suffering, loss, and grieving, I demanded answers from God. *Why? How? Now what?* I pushed and fought hard not to give up control over my life and to maintain my independence. Things had been going so well before this illness. I had felt so mature in my character and my spirit. Growing up, I had acquired a solid base of faith from my mom and from the nuns at the parochial school I had attended for thirteen years. Then I had attended college on a hard-won scholarship, working my way through and graduating with a degree in nursing. I loved my work, my husband, and my new baby. Now my life was in upheaval. I was grappling with the inadequacies of my body and coming to grips with the emotional upset of losing my sense of self.

I didn't see it then, but the upheaval was actually the tilling of soil, the tearing down of weeds, and the laying down of new ground for a fresh start. Like the man lowered through the roof to receive healing (Mark 2:1-12), I was taken up by my friends and brought to Jesus' feet through healing masses, prayer groups, and Bible studies. Where I once felt completely whole and independent, I now realized I was just a part and member of Christ's Body.

Scripture, homilies, and the wisdom of others carried insight to my questions; they became God's voice. But I still didn't know why I was suffering. Why did my life have to involve so much physical pain? I pored over readings related to suffering and illness, feeling especially drawn to the gospel accounts of Christ's healing miracles. It was healing for the body that I wanted; I was not yet ready to hear God's call to healing and growth of the spirit.

Still, I pursued God through prayer, meditation, and other ways—something I hadn't done in my previous healthful state. I had been a good person who was kind to others and spoke to God every day. Now, stripped of my career, self-image, and former standing in my family and community, I made the choice to cling to God.

That's when I discovered St. Paul's words, "Now I rejoice in my sufferings for your sake, and in my flesh I complete what is lacking in Christ's afflictions" (Colossians 1:24). I struggled with this statement for quite a while. How could I offer my suffering? How could it benefit anyone? What possibly could be "lacking" in Christ's suffering? But even as I struggled to understand these words, I held on to them like a lifeline, sometimes gasping and gulping for air in a sea of physical pain and self-pity. I began to make choices—not only to talk to God but to listen, not only to see others as needing God's mercy but to see myself in need as well. Gradually, I heard God's call through St. Paul: what was lacking in Christ's sufferings was my free will.

It struck me that Christ freely took up his cross and died for each one of us. There were no bitter complaints about his lot in life or about "unfairness" in an imperfect world. Jesus *chose* to follow the Father's will—but he won't make that choice for us. Gifted with free will, each of us must accept God's plan for us with humility and openness. While this doesn't necessarily mean giving up hope of a cure or relief from a situation, it does mean living the present moment with a willingness to learn and see God in a whole new light.

For me, this choice has meant rejecting the temptation to become bitter or to entertain the thought of early death. As I have tried to see what God might be teaching me through this unexpected path, I find myself more in tune with other people's inner feelings and motivations. I have become less judgmental and more compassionate, especially towards people I used to think had brought their suffering on themselves. I've learned that just listening to others when you can do nothing else for them can be a valuable service. Most of all, I've learned that God has great and wonderful plans of which we can't even begin to conceive.

At times, I still feel the heaviness of my cross. I see how it weighs down not just me but those I love, who help me to carry it. But always, I remember St. Paul's call to make up in my suffering what Christ is lacking. Now I choose to suffer, thanking God for what I have been given and for the journey he has set before me. Were it not for this "questionable gift," I would not be who I am and would not know and love him so much.

That's Me!
By Lucy Thaddeus
Alsip, Illinois

Then one of them, when he saw that he was healed, turned back, praising God with a loud voice. (Luke 17:15)

Although I considered myself a Catholic, I did not attend Mass very often, and my prayer life left much to be desired. Then God got my attention. I was diagnosed with inoperable lung cancer. This was fourteen years ago.

The priest at the hospital heard my confession. When I was able, I would attend Mass. I held on to my rosary for dear life and focused on the sorrowful mysteries, placing myself at the foot of the cross with our Blessed Mother and Mary Magdalene and begging God's forgiveness. Our Lady's scapular became part of my attire.

Now, when the parable of the ten lepers is read, the tears stream down my face and I say, "Jesus, that's me! I'm back. *I* am the one thanking you."

A Walk in the Woods
By Sharon Rose*

Behold, I am making all things new. (Revelation 21:5)

The air was crisp and clean, scrubbed by the night's rain. All creation seemed to be in celebration of a new day. Genesis, a new beginning—how I longed for it! Alone in a cabin in an autumn woods, I rejoiced for the gift of a retreat, this time of solitude.

As I left the cabin for a sunrise walk, three romping deer stopped to observe me warily. Deciding I was harmless, they resumed their joyful frolic and continued their search for food. The tree-lined path, brilliant in color, sloped downward toward an isolated beach on the James River. Twisting and turning, the path was a reminder of how my life seemed to flow of late. As the sun rose, rays of light shimmered across gentle waves.

Grateful prayer bubbled up easily. "It is so good to be here in your presence, Lord, witnessing your continual unfolding of creation." I felt washed and cleansed from worldly concerns, free to be free, even if only for a few hours. I sensed that I too was being created anew by the Master Creator who lovingly shapes every experience in my life, fashioning me into his likeness.

It took somewhat more effort to make the return ascent. A noise from above caught my attention. A tiny squirrel leapt from branch to branch on the topmost tips of the trees. Again, my thoughts turned heavenward in praise. "Every bit of this wood is alive with your creative love!"

Back at the cabin, I sat in a rocking chair on the rustic porch and continued to enjoy this unfolding spectacle of creation. My attention was caught by a single leaf cascading slowly downward to the earth. It floated about two feet above the ground, swaying and twirling as if keeping time to the music of a song only it heard. I had the impression that the tiny leaf was dancing in praise.

I sat observing the leaf for at least ten minutes, waiting for it to complete its descent. Then impatience took over. I walked to the leaf and plucked it from mid-air. I noticed that it was dried and worn, its original bright green changed to a dark brownish orange. But the withered leaf had continued to dance for joy, as if held by an invisible hand.

I suddenly realized how worn I had become. The death of a relative, battling for the rights of a child with special needs, two daughters off to college, and midlife changes had colored my attitude—but not with peace and joy. It had become challenging to be grateful.

Yet as I held that withered leaf, I also realized that I had grown spiritually throughout the many changes of the seasons. Our heavenly Father who orders all things was holding me by his invisible hand of love, his gaze ever upon me. As demonstrated in the natural world I had been admiring, it is God's nature to create and re-create in love, making all that he creates to resemble himself. I realized that although I age physically, although I may feel worn,

I am being made new by the grace of his creative love.

Loving Creator, I am so grateful for your creative love at work in the experiences of my life. I praise you for continually making all things new—even *me*!

A pseudonym has been used at the author's request.

The Journey to Christmas
By Esperanza Calderon
Chicago, Illinois

Glory to God in the highest heaven, and on earth peace among those whom he favors! (Luke 2:14)

Ever since I was a little girl of about six or seven, I recall our family celebrating the traditional *posadas* prior to Christmas. The *posadas* are nine days of prayers, songs, and festivities commemorating Mary and Joseph's journey to Bethlehem. This custom has its origins in Mexico.

This tradition of the *posadas* continued in our family until our parents passed away. Then it came to a halt. For several years, there were no *posadas*, nothing to help us anticipate the birth of Jesus. To be sure, there were colorful decorations, sparkling lights, Christmas trees.... Still, something was missing. I felt an emptiness, a sadness.

Then one Advent season, I felt something stirring. A thought occurred to me, and I'm sure that the Holy Spirit was instrumental in planting it in my mind. *Why can't I begin the tradition of the posadas once again?* I mentioned the subject to my husband and older children. They reacted with surprise but were eager to renew the tradition. A bit uncertain about how to begin, I enlisted the help of a dear sister-in-law. She was from Mexico, and was truly excited to help.

Much work went into the preparations. We had to decide who would play the Holy Family, what they would wear, and how we would represent their long journey. We prepared the areas they would visit, including a small platform where they would rest. We collected Spanish prayer books and hymns, as well as candles for the procession. Then there was the food—candies and fruit, a piñata full of treats for the children, and tamales for the late evening meal.

That Christmas—the most joyful I have ever experienced—was deeply significant for me and my whole family. We have continued the tradition, and the celebration of Christmas has become full of special meaning for us once again. Each year beginning on December 16, we gather at my home to prepare for the holy event. On the day of our first *posada,* the families begin arriving in their Sunday best, carrying bundles filled with treats which they will later share. The festivities culminate on Christmas Eve with a special ritual called *El Acostamiento*, when the Baby Jesus is rocked before being placed in the manger.

So much joy and love are expressed during our family *posadas* that Christmas Eve finds us ready to join the heavenly angels in announcing the good news of Jesus' birth! We know that we, too, have reason to raise our voices in praise, saying, "Glory to God in the highest!" (Luke 2:14).

May these *posadas* be my legacy to my children, grandchildren, and great-grandchildren.

A Wandering Sheep Comes Home
By Michael Ho
Kuala Lumpur, Malaysia

For thus says the Lord GOD: I myself will search for my sheep, and will seek them out.... I will seek the lost, and I will bring back the strayed. (Ezekiel 34:11, 16)

I was baptized a Catholic just six months before my wife and I were married, in August 1961. For fourteen years following my baptism, I was a nominal Catholic and never bothered to deepen my faith. Not surprisingly, I suffered a terrible fall in my faith life. I started to accompany two Buddhist friends who took regular trips to the northern part of the country to worship a Thai monk. My purpose in going was to obtain from this monk some supernatural powers or charms that would improve my sales of life insurance.

I never did see any improvement in my insurance sales. Neither did I see that I was like a lost sheep; I had fallen into a dark valley, where I risked losing my soul. I have no doubt that the merciful Lord was watching and protecting me as I strayed. After about a year, he came to rescue me through the person of the parish priest—the same one who had instructed me for baptism. The priest invited me to join a newly formed lay ministry that required attending a number of training sessions. I accepted.

It was through those sessions that my Good Shepherd rescued me. Finally, I realized my folly and repented of having wandered along dark ways. The Lord not only brought me back into his sheepfold. During a preaching mission led by a priest from Ireland, he also healed me of gout. It was a total healing of body, soul, and spirit that left me wanting to praise and worship almighty God and to serve him with my whole heart. Ever since, I have tried to live in a way that expresses my gratitude.

In July 1996, some twenty years after God intervened in my life, I found a new way to declare my thanks in words. It happened while I was attending an intensive Catholic Bible study course in Bombay, India. One of the lecturers gave us the assignment of composing a personal psalm of praise and thanksgiving. At first, I was not sure how to approach this project, but after I prayed for awhile, several biblical texts came to mind and my thoughts started flowing. I was especially inspired by two passages about God as the Good Shepherd—Ezekiel 34:11-16 and John 10:1-30. Here is what I wrote:

O Lord, I thank you for your steadfast love and your salvation!
I was born into a family where neither my father nor my mother knew you.
With your love and your care, I grew up to be a young man.

It was then that I glimpsed the first sign of your love for me through the love of a young woman.
I fell in love with her, and to marry her,
I was baptized into this universal Church.

But my bond with you did not last long.
Soon I began to forsake you and to worship false gods.
But you are a God who is slow to anger
and full of steadfast love and mercy for me, a sinner!

Even though I had betrayed you,
you watched over me constantly, lest I be lost forever.
You allowed me to stray for only a year.

Then, as a Good Shepherd, you found me, carried me on your shoulders
and brought me safely back to your sheepfold.

There you nursed me with your tender love and your
boundless mercy.
You even healed me of a painful disease that had afflicted
me for more than ten long years!

O Lord, you are a great God! You not only healed me of my
physical sickness—
you also made me whole in my total person!

Since then, you have changed my entire life.
I want to praise you and thank you,
to love and serve you
with all my mind, all my heart, all my soul, and all my
strength!

Your love and mercy endure forever!
Praise the Lord, O my soul,
for he is my Lord and my Savior.
Alleluia!

The Gifts That Last
By Ludy Z. Pardo
Las Piñas City, Philippines

Daughter, your faith has made you well; go in peace, and be healed of your disease. (Mark 5:34)

Two years ago, after consulting a specialist about the lower back and leg pain I had been experiencing, I was told that I needed spinal surgery immediately. Since I was heavily involved in planning a big international conference at the Asian Development Bank, where I work, I tried to put off the operation. The doctor cautioned against it. He warned that if my condition deteriorated, I risked becoming paralyzed.

Resigning myself to the inevitable, I asked my family and friends to pray for a successful outcome. I received exceptional support from fellow members of a Catholic renewal movement for business people and professionals; these brothers and sisters in the Lord expressed their love and care in many ways.

As I was praying a few days before the operation, Jesus spoke to me through the gospel story of the woman with a hemorrhage. I felt his words addressed to me: "Daughter, your faith has made you well; go in peace, and be healed of your disease" (Mark 5:34). That night in the hospital room, several people from the movement prayed over me, asking for God's protection, a successful operation, and complete recovery.

February 1 was the big day. I was wheeled into the operating room around 7:00 a.m. and was prepared for surgery by the anesthesiologist. That was the last thing I remember. When I regained consciousness, I thought the medical staff was still waiting for the surgeon. Only when I touched my back and felt thick bandages did I realize that the operation was over.

To my surprise, my recovery was amazingly fast. I took my first ten steps while still in the hospital and was ecstatic! My fear of being paralyzed vanished, and I felt God's reassuring care. But the evil one was at work, too. One incident that took place during this time was a particular temptation against faith and gratefulness to God.

Taking advantage of my family's preoccupation with my recovery, a gang of robbers phoned our home while my husband, Lito, was at work. They spoke to our house helpers and convinced them that Lito had met with an accident, was being detained by the police, and needed money. Our helpers responded to this seeming emergency by following what they thought were Lito's instructions to collect all our jewelry and cash and deliver it to someone at a certain location. They were thorough—we even lost our wedding rings.

When Lito learned what had happened, he was especially concerned about how I would react, given my fragile physical condition. By God's grace, I took the news quite well. Later that night, as I prayed about it, the Lord spoke to me clearly: He reminded me that material things bring temporary joy and can be taken away quickly, and that I had received the lasting and immeasurable joy of his love and healing. I felt overwhelmed by God's great goodness and even more grateful for his gifts. "The devil cannot snatch this victory of healing from me," I firmly declared.

Now, like the woman in Mark 5, I too "go in peace ... healed of [my] disease." Fully recovered from my back problems, I continue to count my blessings. I thank God for restoring my failing body, for enabling me to wiggle my toes, move around, stand up and walk again—all without any pain or discomfort. I thank him for family and friends, but especially for my renewed sense of security in his love and protection. God is indeed the greatest healer!

12

Walking by Faith

Every day we put our faith in a whole multitude of unseen realities that make ordinary life possible. We flip a light switch with the expectation that the electrician, the power company, and the light bulb manufacturer have done their work. We set a glass on the counter—an unconscious expression of faith in the law of gravity. If we are healthy, we take it for granted that our hearts will beat and our lungs will take in air without our having to think about it.

The contributors to this chapter point to another type of unseen reality—those critical, behind-the-scenes truths by which Jesus invites us to live. Their stories highlight various ways in which God's word helps us to put our faith in Jesus and in the inheritance he won for us by his life, death, and resurrection.

The Letter to the Hebrews tells us that "faith is the assurance of things hoped for, the conviction of things not seen" (Hebrews 11:1). Walking by faith means journeying through life with the One who has promised us our wonderful inheritance. It means trusting that he is in control, even when our life circumstances seem to say the opposite. It means knowing he is present with us, even when we cannot see him.

"The LORD is good to those who wait for him, to the soul that seeks him," Scripture says (Lamentations 3:25). Let's seek him wholeheartedly. Let's continue our journey of faith with the attitude St. Bernard of Clairvaux recommends: "Seek the Lord by your prayers, seek him by your actions. Find him by your faith. What is there that faith does not find? It attains the unreachable, it discovers the hidden, grasps the immeasurable, embraces the farthest depths." Lord, we put our faith in you!

Think About It!

John Henry Newman wrote the following expression of faith during a time of great personal distress and darkness, but it's a good word for any season of life:

> God has created me to do him some definite service. He has committed some work to me which he has not committed to any other. I have my mission. I may never know it in this life, but I shall be told it in the next. Somehow, I am necessary for his purposes.... God has not created me for nothing. I shall do good. I shall do his work. I shall be an angel of peace, a preacher of truth in my own place, ... if only I keep his commandments and serve him in my calling. Therefore I will trust him.... He knows what he is about. (*Meditations and Devotions*)

Pray It!

We walk by faith, not by sight. (2 Corinthians 5:7)

Jesus said to him, "If you are able!—All things can be done for the one who believes." Immediately the father of the child cried out, "I believe; help my unbelief!" (Mark 9:23-24)

Last-Minute Save

By Kathleen Hervochon
Damariscotta, Maine

I have been crucified with Christ; it is no longer I who live, but Christ who lives in me. (Galatians 2:20)

My husband George and I were overjoyed when we realized we were expecting our third child. We marveled once again at God's goodness and provision for us. The pregnancy caused us to reflect on how God had led us to make a major life change right after we attended a Marriage Encounter weekend retreat seven years before. Believing that God was directing us, we had left family and friends behind in our hometowns in New Jersey and moved to New England with our daughters—four-year-old Gwyn and ten-month-old AnniPat—in tow.

Without any definite prospects for employment, we settled in a small Maine town where neither of us had ever lived. George, formerly a broker on Wall Street, built our home with his own hands. We were immediately welcomed with open arms into a tiny but vibrant Catholic parish. Our spirituality as a young little family deepened, while our church community became the nucleus of our lives. George began building homes as a profession. Even the skeptical family members we had left behind in New Jersey began to see God's hand in our decision to move.

We awaited the birth of our next child with great joy and anticipation. Although this pregnancy was threatened by toxemia and possible premature delivery, our third precious daughter, Megan, was delivered on her original due date. We again recognized God's goodness in her healthy birth, and couldn't wait to share our love with her.

Unexpectedly, in the weeks that followed, I had great difficulty sleeping and found myself becoming uncharacteristically irritable and depressed. I consulted my obstetrician, with the expectation that she would offer words of comfort and assurance that these days of darkness would soon disappear in thin air. She didn't. To my shock and horror, she referred me to a psychiatrist. Ten minutes into the visit, the psychiatrist diagnosed me with severe postpartum depression and arranged for my admittance into the psychiatric unit of a nearby hospital.

My husband drove me straight to the hospital, and then went home to get my new infant. Megan would stay with me in the hospital. Because I was put on a tranquilizer and an antidepressant, however, I had to stop nursing her. I felt caught in a nightmare. How could this be happening? Megan and I remained in the hospital for two weeks, but when we returned home, I still felt totally incapacitated. I was useless and felt so ashamed.

Dear friends rallied around my family with meals, offers to babysit, emotional support, and, of course, constant prayer. We hired a woman to come every day from 8:00 a.m. to 4:00 p.m. to care for our daughters and help get me through the day. My helper was a good friend. She ushered me out the door each morning to attend Mass, though I would have preferred to stay sheltered and "safe" in my home. She also insisted that I needed exercise and instructed me to walk as far as the huge old oak tree that sprawled over the edge of the road. As I reached this destination each day, I would press my back against the trunk of the tree, lift my head to peer through the enormous outstretched branches, and recite the *Glory Be*. I then walked the mile home. I called this huge oak my "Glory Be Tree." With each journey there, I tried to offer the most sincere, heartfelt *Glory Be* I had ever uttered.

Despite medication and endless hours of counseling, I felt little relief. My feelings of inadequacy and worthlessness continued to multiply. Weeks of desperation turned into months; months turned into two years. I was referred from one doctor to the next, as each course of treatment failed. I underwent twelve electric shock therapy treatments and spent a total of eight months as a psychiatric patient in three different hospitals. Friends remained supportive but had become weary, and my family was all but shattered.

During this time of great turmoil, I desperately sought comfort and relief from God's word. I memorized Bible quotes: "I keep the LORD always before me; because he is at my right hand, I shall not be moved" (Psalm 16:8). "May the God of hope fill you with all joy and peace in believing, so that you may abound in hope by the power of the Holy Spirit" (Romans 15:13). These verses played over and over again in my mind and heart. Many times I cried out to God, asking, "Where are you now, when I need you most?"

I was struggling with my circumstances and God's apparent indifference, when an image gradually took shape in my mind. I did not see this image outside myself. It was displayed on an interior stage, at eye level, when I was still and quiet. Gradually I identified the vision as Christ's crucifixion. I became intensely engrossed in his suffering. I was absorbed in his agony. Then, little by little, the features on the face of Christ began to change. Slowly I recognized my face transposed over his. The impression of my face interchanging with the face of Christ resembled the alternating appearance of a hologram. Greatly disturbed by what I saw, I screamed out my protest to God. I rebelled at the depth of the pain he seemed to be asking me to bear. But over a period of weeks, I came to a reluctant understanding of the image. I began to comprehend "shared suffering." Jesus was telling me that he knew and felt my pain.

My suffering did not diminish, but I was strengthened by this profound communication. I revealed it to no one, for fear I would be told I was hallucinating.

But my depression continued on, unrelenting, and I began to

find comfort in the thought of ending my depression by ending my life. At 2:00 a.m. one September morning in 1984, armed with an arsenal of previously prescribed drugs and a jug of water, I started toward the door to venture deep into the woods behind my home. I reasoned that by the time my family woke and found me, my intentions would be carried out. Before I opened the door I prayed, "God, I am giving you one chance to stop me." My Bible was on the table next to the door, and I felt led to open it. My eyes fell on Galatians 2:20:

> I have been crucified with Christ; it is no longer I who live, but Christ who lives in me; and the life I now live in the flesh I live by faith in the Son of God, who loved me and gave himself for me.

I was stunned. The words confirmed my vision. They convinced me that killing myself could not destroy my inner core, which was anchored in Christ. But I had to live a life of *faith* in the Son of God who died on the cross and who knew my pain so thoroughly. I could not have the audacity to treat God's gracious gift as pointless (Galatians 2:21).

I returned to my bed and fell fast asleep. The next morning, I shared with my husband how God's hand led me miraculously to a Scripture that kept me from taking my life. I told George how directly God's word spoke to me in that hour of desperation—it was as alive and active as it was to St. Paul when he wrote it. Both of us were awed at the realization that God's word does not return to him empty, but accomplishes his will.

My depression remained with me for five more years, with some days being better than others. But throughout those years, I remained very firmly convinced that suicide was not an option. Because God led me to Galatians 2 at a very pivotal moment, I could easily believe in his divine love and intervention. Jesus gave me a vision to show me that my suffering was linked with his and to assure that, like him, I would rise again.

Rough Seas, Good Sailing
By Joseph Komban
Cochin, Kerala, India

Let not your hearts be troubled; believe in God,
believe also in me. (John 14:1)

Early in my life, my parents gave me the nickname Simon—in Malayalam, our mother tongue, this means "son of the sea." As it turned out, I graduated with a degree in mechanical engineering and then began a career as a marine engineer working on ships. My work took me to many countries, but I discovered that the sailor's life did not appeal to me. The problem was that I got seasick very easily. When the waves started dancing, so did my stomach.

A classmate had given me a Bible that I always carried on board when I sailed. In it I kept a holy card of Jesus that I especially liked because his eyes seemed so loving. Every time I prayed, I would look at that picture and ask God for work that wouldn't require having to go to sea.

After about fifteen years, I decided it was time for a career change. There is a fishing harbor very near my home. I had observed it closely and had made a careful study of the local fishing industry. Since it appeared to be an interesting and lucrative business, I decided to build a fishing boat, hire a captain and crew, and launch my own company. Even though this meant taking out a bank loan and pledging my property as collateral, I wasn't worried. Prospects were good. The fishing industry was doing so well that I expected to be able to build a second boat within a year. With very great hopes, I launched my fishing trawler into the blue waters of the Arabian Sea. The waves seemed to dance and jump as the boat slid into the water.

Every day I kept a careful eye on the catch. It wasn't bad at first, but then it began declining. To my great distress, I saw that many boats were now returning to harbor with empty fish-holds. Months passed, and the catch became very poor. Where had the fish gone? Embarrassment, worry, anxiety, despair—all these emotions pressed down on me as I stood in the harbor looking out at the sea. Now those small waves seemed to be dancing against me, frustrating my dreams.

With no income, I worried about my family's welfare. What would we live on? How would I pay back the loan? I looked at my fishing trawler, now tied up near the jetty and felt lost in a sort of Bermuda Triangle from which there was no escape.

Feeling a need for more prayer than usual, I was inspired to spend some nights in continuous prayer to the Lord. One night, an intuition came to me to just open the Bible and read whatever I might find. I remembered that St. Augustine had done this in a moment of great anguish just before his conversion. With a fervent mental prayer, I opened my Bible and began reading these lines: "Let not your hearts be troubled; believe in God, believe also in me" (John 14:1). The words struck me forcefully. It was as if the Lord Jesus were standing there speaking directly to me—bringing me gifts of peace, faith, and hope. His loving eyes were truly upon me.

Two weeks later, through a friend's efforts, I was invited to interview for a promising job in a country in the Persian Gulf. My wife and I agreed that I should go to the interview and leave fishing behind. Things fell into place. I sold my trawler to the boat's captain and crew, then set out for Bombay, my departure point for the Gulf. But I never got to the interview. In Bombay, my briefcase was stolen. With it I lost my passport, money, important documents—and, of course, that promising job.

As shaken and shattered as I felt, I held onto that scriptural command to "believe in God" and in Jesus. The verse became a prayer that helped me maintain faith, fight despair, and receive God's peace during those difficult days. Over and over I would pray, "Yes, Lord, I have confidence in you!" I saw little "miracles" too—like being able to obtain replacement documents in just a fraction of the time I had expected.

Soon after that, another employment possibility came my way. When I looked into it, this one didn't seem so promising. It was from a company that was running huge losses. Since the prospects for reviving it seemed very slim, I was very reluctant to accept the offer.

While I was still deliberating about what to do, I had a dream. I was in a room with many other people. Each of us was given a try at opening a small box. Everyone was unsuccessful—until that small box came to me. I took it in my hands and opened it with the greatest ease. The dream was so vivid and unusual that I took it as a sign. Perhaps that struggling company was my "small box"! Perhaps I could succeed at reversing its decline. I decided to accept the job. After only one year, the company was making a profit.

One thing I have learned from all this: Whatever waves and storms may come, we will sail with untroubled heart on the sea of life if only we accept Jesus' invitation to "believe in God, believe also in me."

His Mercy Is Always Near
By Doris Biel Herter
Louisville, Kentucky

Let us then approach the throne of grace with confidence, so that we may receive mercy and find grace to help us in our time of need. (Hebrews 4:16, NIV)

Twenty years ago, I was shocked to learn that my twelve-year-old daughter, Jennifer, had a threatening tissue growth that had spread into her jaw. I was told that her right jawbone would have to be removed; bone taken from her hip would be used to replace it.

Jennifer is the youngest of our six children. When she was only fifteen months old, her father was diagnosed with cancer. His death left me raising the children alone. It was a traumatic time in our lives, but by the grace of God, we all got through the tragedy and continued on with life. And now, just ten years later, here was another unexpected and sobering diagnosis. I really struggled with it. "Why is this happening to such a gentle, sweet, and kind little girl?" I asked the Lord.

Overwhelmed with sorrow and apprehension, Jennifer and I traveled from Kentucky to California, where the surgery was to be performed. The day before the surgery, as I sat with her in the hospital room, I took out an issue of *The Word Among Us* that I had brought from home. What I was really searching for were answers for my troubled soul and help for Jennifer.

I opened the magazine and read the Scripture passage and meditation for the day. Exactly what it said, I don't recall. But I do remember that I responded by desperately calling on the Holy Spirit and asking for peace and healing for Jennifer. As I put the magazine down, I was enveloped by a complete assurance that

God was with us. For the first time since learning about my daughter's condition, I was feeling the peace and love of God. I walked over to the bed, laid my hands on Jennifer and prayed, assuring her that everything was going to be okay.

And indeed it was. The surgery was a success. When I thanked the surgeon and told him our family had been praying, he informed me that the entire medical staff had been doing the same. Today, Jennifer is married and has a beautiful little girl of her own.

As I see it, what happened that day in Jennifer's hospital room is described in Hebrews 4:16: Boldly I approach the throne of God to obtain mercy and grace for help in time of need. Before I could do that, though, I needed a little nudge—which is what I received when I opened *The Word Among Us* to read the word of God and open myself to the presence of the Holy Spirit. Then his peace encompassed my whole being so that I was able to encourage my daughter and be there for her.

What did I learn from this experience? I learned that God is always with us and that his throne of grace is very near. I realized that he is always waiting for us to ask for and receive his grace and help for every situation. Through all these years since the surgery, I have tried to do just that. I come to God often—and I have rarely missed a day reading the Scriptures.

Together Forever
By Sylvia Jean*

In Christ all will be brought to life. (1 Corinthians 15:22, NJB)

This is a Scripture verse that has given me great comfort in the loss of my mother, who died of cancer a few years ago. We were very close. I have a prayer card with these words printed on it, along with a picture of the risen Christ coming upon the clouds with arms upraised, with a glowing cross in the background. It always turns my thoughts to the resurrection and the Second Coming.

It is very consoling to know we can look forward to eternal life. So many have gone before me. As I meditate on my prayer card and its message, I grow in faith that I will live with them again some day, in eternal happiness with our dear Savior—this time never to be separated again.

In Christ all will come to life again. Amen! Praise God!

Pseudonym used at the author's request.

Too Many Riches?
By John Mitchell
Falls Church, Virginia

It is easier for a camel to go through the eye of a needle than for someone who is rich to enter the kingdom of God.
(Mark 10:25)

Life's important memories come complete with an extraordinary assortment of details that help to underscore them in our minds. When I think of the life memory that influenced my decision to pursue teaching as a career, I can still remember the color of the bedspread I had at the time. It was light brown with bold lines of red, blue, and yellow crisscrossing the entire area.

I was lying on that bedspread—a young boy entering my preteen years—when I read this line from Scripture: "It is easier for a camel to go through the eye of a needle than for someone who is rich to enter the kingdom of God" (Mark 10:25). I became concerned about my salvation.

I knew that my family was not poor. We were never hungry. We were able to drive to visit our extended family for any holiday. Santa was generous at Christmas. My siblings and I felt loved by both of our parents. I didn't know anyone who lived in any better circumstances. I felt pretty rich compared with other children I had heard about. Was I rich enough to have trouble getting into heaven?

I wanted very much to be in heaven with God someday. However, the eye of a sewing needle is pretty tiny. There must be something more to this Scripture verse than I understood. I wondered if I should forsake the riches that I experienced growing up to help assure that I could be with God someday. I thought about going to a faraway place to be a missionary.

My grandmother had just purchased a color television, the first one I had ever seen. She was a very holy woman. I realized then that some good people had things my family did not have. Those things did not seem extremely important to me, but should they affect how I planned my life? Should I try to make enough money to enjoy those nicer things? Was the eye of a needle a little bigger than I had thought?

By the time I was in college, many of my acquaintances were very interested in careers that would generate high incomes. I looked around and realized that many of these people were very good people and that they were not necessarily forsaking their salvation for money. But I did believe that they might be setting up obstacles to their salvation, as Jesus had warned about. I didn't want to follow that road.

During this period of my life, I took some time off from school. When I returned to college, I worked as an intern in public schools.

I realized then that I would be very happy working with young people. I decided to become a public school teacher. Maybe this would even have a bearing on my salvation, I thought. Public school teachers are not noted for being rich!

I did not make my career choice based solely on this Scripture verse, but my value system has certainly been shaped by the "eye of a needle." I sometimes think of that day in my youth when I was on my bed reading Scripture. I wonder if I have become too influenced by "riches," even as a teacher. What I want and what I need might not always be what God wants for me or what he knows I need.

One of my prayers to God continues to be for help in this area of my life. More than ever, I desire to be with him always.

A Mustard Seed for Chris
By Sharon George*

If you have faith the size of a mustard seed, ... nothing will be impossible for you. (Matthew 17:20)

My son Chris has had drug problems for many years. He has been suicidal and has been in treatment centers and jails. As a mother, this has been extremely hard for me. My first husband left me in the hospital when Chris was born. I raised him alone for eleven years.

I have felt a lot of guilt. When Chris has been homeless or completely out of contact for extended periods of time, I have constantly prayed to God to wrap his protection around him and to put an angel in his life to help him. These words help me: "He will command his angels concerning you to guard you in all your ways" (Psalm 91:11). And when I pray that my husband and I will receive the strength and wisdom to help Chris in whatever ways we can, these words help me too: "I hereby command you: Be strong and courageous; do not be frightened or dismayed, for the LORD your God is with you wherever you go" (Joshua 1:9).

I know that as long as my son is alive, there is hope. So especially, I hang on to Jesus' promise that "if you have faith the size of a mustard seed ... nothing will be impossible for you" (Matthew 17:20). With God nothing is impossible—certainly not the rescue of a wayward son.

Pseudonym used at the author's request.

Leigh Anne's Verse
By Davin Winger
Gruver, Texas

If you believe, you will receive whatever you ask for in prayer.
(Matthew 21:22, NIV)

Boy, was I in a hurry! I had been working on the farm all day. It was corn-planting season, with plenty to do. I came home and took a quick shower, hurrying to get to a prayer meeting about the community Bible study that was going on in our town. Before running out the door, I looked in on our five-year-old, Leigh Anne. There she lay on her bed with her legs crossed, reading a small children's King James Bible.

I asked, " Leigh Anne, what are you doing?" She hadn't learned to read yet, and this Bible didn't have many pictures.

"I'm looking to see if this Bible has my verse," she said matter of factly. When she told me what "her" verse was, I was amazed at how well it described what was going on in my life at the time. First, some background.

My spiritual life had literally exploded in the past year. I was raised in a small rural Church of Christ and had come back home to farm with my dad after college. I am so thankful to the people in that church for introducing me to Jesus and giving me a familiarity with the Scriptures.

From very early on, God planted in me a desire for all believers in Jesus to come together in his name. Six years ago, God began to make this a reality for me. I attended a "Walk to Emmaus," a Methodist version of a Catholic Cursillo renewal weekend, with believers in Jesus from many different backgrounds—Baptist, Catholic, Methodist, Lutheran, charismatic. I was experiencing the Body of Christ in a big way. I was also experiencing the presence of the Holy Spirit in my life. God poured out his Holy Spirit on me, and for many months after that weekend, I felt this "cloud" around me. I became more alert to the Spirit's workings and found myself talking about Jesus to people I would never have expected.

The following spring, a friend of mine had the vision to start a Bible study. What he had in mind was studying the Book of Proverbs with some local teens. The kicker was that he also envisioned the parents participating and mentoring their children as they worked on the Bible study together, which would lead them to talk about issues such as drinking, drugs, sex, and peer pressure.

The Lord had made the town ripe for such a thing, and many wanted to participate. Before we knew it, we had Baptists, Catholics, Methodists, Church of Christ, First Christian, and Lutherans working side by side to make this study a reality. Parents and teens signed up, and teens whose parents weren't able to participate were paired with adult volunteers. We were thinking that about forty girls and forty boys would come, along with their mentors. Just to be on the safe side, we prepared for sixty of each and bought what we thought was an ample supply of notebooks, Bibles, and marker pens.

Our Father in heaven had a different idea. The first night of the Bible study, about 160 teens showed up—eighty "P-31 Girls" (we named their group after the "capable woman" of Proverbs 31) and eighty "Wise Guys"—along with parents and other mentors. People were lined up at the door trying to get in. A person couldn't find a parking place on Main Street—which never happens in Gruver! I was dumbfounded. God had truly given us more than we could imagine.

In addition to the people involved in the actual Bible study, a dozen adults usually gathered to pray for the teens, parents, and other mentors as they were meeting. The town had come together in the name of Jesus, and people were noticing. By the end of that six-week study of Proverbs, over two hundred people had become involved in one way or other. We had to move out of the way because God was coming through!

We were in the middle of that Bible study the night I found Leigh Anne looking for "her" verse. In fact, I was headed out the door for a meeting where some of us were coming together to plan and pray for it.

"So what's your verse, Leigh Anne?"

"Matthew 21:22," she tells me. "If you believe you will receive whatever you ask for in prayer."

Here I was going to a prayer meeting, and God was telling me through my little girl that he was in the prayer-answering business! I went to that meeting and shared the story with my friends. Together, we gave thanks to God for all that he had done.

On Easter 2001 I found myself being confirmed into the Catholic Church. As I look back, I can see God's leading me there from the moment I met my wife, Teague, and went to my first

Catholic Mass with her family. Yet the path has not always been smooth, and I questioned the Church and myself at many turns.

One hurdle that I had to cross was the Real Presence of Christ in the Eucharist. I couldn't figure out how God changed the bread and wine into the Body and the Blood of Christ. As I was thinking about this problem of mine, a Scripture verse came to me. It was Leigh Anne's verse again: "If you believe you will receive whatever you ask for in prayer."

God had broken through to me. When the priest prays the Eucharistic Prayer, our Father answers. His answers aren't contingent on my belief, or even that of the priest. (In my limited experience of attending Mass, however, the belief of the priest and the parishioners in the Real Presence of Christ in the Eucharist is evident to me.)

One day I asked Leigh Anne how she had known about Matthew 21:22. She said she learned it at "Kids for Christ," an after-school youth program at the local Methodist church. I still long for the day when all believers will come together in the name of Jesus. Who knows? Maybe God will use my children and their generation to accomplish such a thing.

For myself, I pray that all believers in Jesus might come to Jesus through the Eucharist. And once again I remind myself that "if you believe, you will receive."

Topical Index of Scripture Verses

The Scripture passages singled out by the people who contributed to this book can help you in your own prayer life. Many of these verses are listed here, grouped into themes for your convenience.

God's Love

If my father and mother forsake me,
the LORD will take me up.
— Psalm 27:10

For I am convinced that neither death, nor life, ... nor anything else in all creation, will be able to separate us from the love of God in Christ Jesus our Lord.
—Romans 8:38,39

The LORD is my shepherd,
I shall not want.
—Psalm 23:1

The one who enters by the gate is the shepherd of the sheep. The gatekeeper opens the gate for him, and the sheep hear his voice. He calls his own sheep by name and leads them out. When he has brought out all his own, he goes ahead of them, and the sheep follow him because they know his voice. They will not follow a stranger, but they will run from him because they do not know the voice of strangers.
—John 10:2-5

I trusted in your steadfast love;
my heart shall rejoice in your salvation.
I will sing to the LORD,
because he has dealt bountifully with me.
—Psalm 13:5-6

I pray that you may have the power to comprehend, with
all the saints, what is the breadth and length and height
and depth, and to know the love of Christ that surpasses
knowledge, so that you may be filled with all the fullness
of God.
—Ephesians 3:18-19

We know love by this, that he laid down his life for us—
and we ought to lay down our lives for one another.
—1 John 3:16

Good News

He has anointed me to bring good news to the poor.
He has sent me to proclaim release to the captives
and recovery of sight to the blind, to let the oppressed
go free.
—Luke 4:18

I am bringing you good news of great joy for all the people: to you is born this day in the city of David a Savior,
who is the Messiah, the Lord.
—Luke 2:10-11

Then Jesus said to the Jews who had believed in him, "If
you continue in my word, you are truly my disciples; and

you will know the truth, and the truth will make you free.... Very truly, I tell you, everyone who commits sin is a slave to sin.... If the Son makes you free, you will be free indeed."
—John 8:31-32, 34, 36

Come to me, all who labor and are heavy laden, and I will give you rest. Take my yoke upon you, and learn from me; for I am gentle and lowly in heart, and you will find rest for your souls. For my yoke is easy, and my burden is light.
—Matthew 11:28-30

All will be made alive in Christ.
—1 Corinthians 15:22

You did not choose me, but I chose you.
—John 15:16

I shall not die, but I shall live,
and recount the deeds of the LORD.
—Psalm 118:17

I have been crucified with Christ; and it is no longer I who live, but Christ who lives in me; and the life I now live in the flesh I live by faith in the Son of God, who loved me and gave himself for me. I do not nullify the grace of God.
—Galatians 2:20-21

For surely I know the plans I have for you, says the LORD, plans for your welfare and not for harm, to give you a future with hope. Then when you call upon me and come and pray to me, I will hear you. When you search for me, you will find me.
—Jeremiah 29:11-13

Promises to Live By

Awake, O sleeper, and arise from the dead, and Christ shall give you light.
—Ephesians 5:14

My sheep hear my voice. I know them, and they follow me. I give them eternal life, and they will never perish.
—John 10:27-28

For thus says the Lord GOD: I myself will search for my sheep, and will seek them out…. I will seek the lost, and I will bring back the strayed.
—Ezekiel 34:11,16

See, I am making all things new.
—Revelation 21:5

Those who eat my flesh and drink my blood have eternal life, and I will raise them up on the last day.
—John 6:54

With God all things are possible.
—Matthew 19:26

He will command his angels concerning you
to guard you in all your ways.
—Psalm 91:11

We know that all things work together for good for those who love God, who are called according to his purpose.
—Romans 8:28

For thus said the Lord GOD, the Holy One of Israel:
"In returning and rest you shall be saved;
in quietness and in trust shall be your strength."
—Isaiah 30:15

Do not be conformed to this world, but be transformed by the renewing of your minds, so that you may discern what is the will of God—what is good and acceptable and perfect.
—Romans 12:2

Guidance for Living

You are not your own; you were bought with a price. So glorify God in your body.
—1 Corinthians 6:19-20

See to it ... that no root of bitterness springs up and causes trouble.
—Hebrews 12:15

A cheerful heart is a good medicine.
—Proverbs 17:22

Your word is a lamp to my feet
and a light to my path.
—Psalm 119:105

Whatever is true, whatever is honorable, whatever is just, whatever is pure, whatever is pleasing, whatever is commendable, if there is any excellence and if there is anything worthy of praise, think about these things.
—Philippians 4:8

Every scribe who has been trained for the kingdom of
heaven is like a householder who brings out of his treasure
what is new and what is old.
—Matthew 13:52

A fool raises his voice when he laughs,
but the wise smile quietly.
—Sirach 21:20

Strength and dignity are her clothing,
and she laughs at the time to come.
—Proverbs 31:25

Sobering Reminders

Enter through the narrow gate.
—Matthew 7:13

But I tell you that on the day of judgment it will be more
tolerable for the land of Sodom than for you.
—Matthew 11:24

It is easier for a camel to go through the eye of a needle
than for someone who is rich to enter the kingdom of God.
—Mark 10:25

God opposes the proud,
but gives grace to the humble.
—James 4:6

And he sighed deeply in his spirit and said, "Why does this generation ask for a sign? Truly I tell you, no sign will be given to this generation."
—Mark 8:12

Unless you change and become like children, you will never enter the kingdom of heaven.
—Matthew 18:3

To Help You Pray...

• **in praise and thanksgiving**
Bless the LORD, O my soul,
and do not forget all his benefits—
who forgives all your iniquity,
who heals all your diseases,
who redeems your life from the Pit,
who crowns you with steadfast love and mercy.
—Psalm 103:2-4

Then one of them, when he saw that he was healed, turned back, praising God with a loud voice.
—Luke 17:15

He inclined to me and heard my cry.
He drew me up from the desolate pit....
He put a new song in my mouth,
a song of praise to our God.
—Psalm 40:1-2, 3

Our Father who art in heaven,
Hallowed be thy name....
—Matthew 6:9

I will give thanks to the LORD with my whole heart;
I will tell of all your wonderful deeds.
I will be glad and exult in you;
I will sing praise to your name, O Most High.
—Psalm 9:1-2

• in petition
Let us therefore approach the throne of grace with bold-
ness, so that we may receive mercy and find grace to help
in time of need.
—Hebrews 4:16

I lift up my eyes to the hills—
from where will my help come?
My help comes from the LORD,
who made heaven and earth.
—Psalm 121:1-2

I cried out, "Lord, you are my Father;
do not forsake me in the days of trouble....
I will praise your name continually,
and will sing hymns of thanksgiving."
My prayer was heard,
for you saved me from destruction
and rescued me in time of trouble.
For this reason I thank you and praise you,
and I bless the name of the Lord.
—Sirach 51:10, 11-12

Do not worry about anything, but in everything by prayer
and supplication with thanksgiving let your requests be
made known to God. And the peace of God, which surpasses all understanding, will guard your hearts and your
minds in Christ Jesus.
—Philippians 4:6-7

• **for healing**

Do you want to be healed?

—John 5:6

Daughter, your faith has made you well; go in peace, and be healed of your disease.

— Mark 5:34

Honor physicians for their services,
for the Lord created them;
for their gift of healing comes from the Most High.

—Sirach 38:1-2

• **in the right spirit**

Search me, O God, and know my heart;
test me and know my thoughts.
See if there is any wicked way in me,
and lead me in the way everlasting.

—Psalm 139:23-24

Whenever you stand praying, forgive.

—Mark 11:25

Forgive us our debts,
as we also have forgiven our debtors.

—Matthew 6:12

Unless you change and become like children, you will never enter the kingdom of heaven.

—Matthew 18:3

Whatever you ask for in prayer with faith, you will receive.

—Matthew 21:22

I waited patiently for the LORD;
he inclined to me and heard my cry.
—Psalm 40:1

• **always**
Seek the LORD and his strength;
seek his presence continually.
—Psalm 105:4

Rejoice in hope, be patient in suffering, persevere in prayer.
—Romans 12:12

Rejoice always, pray without ceasing, give thanks in all circumstances; for this is the will of God in Christ Jesus for
you.
—1 Thessalonians 5:16-18

When You're Feeling...

• **afraid**
Even the hairs of your head are all counted. So do not be
afraid.
—Matthew 10:30-31

When it was evening on that day, the first day of the week,
and the doors of the house where the disciples had met
were locked for fear of the Jews, Jesus came and stood
among them and said, "Peace be with you."
—John 20:19

You will not fear the terror of the night.
—Psalm 91:5

I hereby command you: Be strong and courageous; do not be frightened or dismayed, for the LORD your God is with you wherever you go."—Joshua 1:9

• **anxious**
Cast all your anxiety on [God], because he cares for you.
—1 Peter 5:7

O our God ... We do not know what to do, but our eyes are on you.
—2 Chronicles 20:12

May the God of hope fill you with all joy and peace in believing, so that you may abound in hope by the power of the Holy Spirit.
—Romans 15:13

Let not your hearts be troubled; believe in God, believe also in me.
—John 14:1

• **alone**
O LORD, you have searched me and known me.
You know when I sit down and when I rise up;
you discern my thoughts from far away.
—Psalm 139:1-2

See that it is I myself. Touch me and see.
—Luke 24:39

Look, the virgin shall conceive and bear a son,
and they shall name him Emmanuel,
which means, "God is with us."
—Matthew 1:23

And remember, I am with you always, to the end of the age.
—Matthew 28:20

When Times Get Tough

In my flesh I am completing what is lacking in Christ's afflictions for the sake of his body, that is, the church.
—Colossians 1:24

My grace is sufficient for you, for my power is made perfect in weakness.
—2 Corinthians 12:9

He did not hide his face from me,
but heard when I cried to him.
—Psalm 22:24

Comfort, O comfort my people,
says your God.
—Isaiah 40:1

The LORD is near to the brokenhearted,
and saves the crushed in spirit.
—Psalm 34:18

Trust and Believe

Go from your country and your kindred and your father's house to the land that I will show you.
—Genesis 12:1

If you have faith the size of a mustard seed, ... nothing will be impossible for you.
—Matthew 17:20

The LORD did for Sarah as he had promised. Sarah conceived and bore Abraham a son in his old age.
—Genesis 21:1-2

We walk by faith, not by sight.
—2 Corinthians 5:7

Jesus said to him, "If you are able!—All things can be done for the one who believes." Immediately the father of the child cried out, "I believe; help my unbelief!"
—Mark 9:23-24

Having the eyes of your heart enlightened, . . . you may know what is the hope to which he has called you.
—Ephesians 1:18

O LORD of hosts, happy is everyone who trusts in you.
—Psalm 84:12

Called to Serve

Now there are varieties of gifts, but the same Spirit; and there are varieties of services, but the same Lord; and there are varieties of activities, but it is the same God who activates all of them in everyone. To each is given the manifestation of the Spirit for the common good.
—1 Corinthians 12:4-7

He sat down, called the twelve, and said to them,
"Whoever wants to be first must be last of all and servant
of all."
—Mark 9:35

If a brother or sister is ill-clad and in lack of daily food,
and one of you says to them, "Go in peace, be warmed and
filled," without giving them the things needed for the body,
what does it profit? So faith by itself, if it has no works, is
dead.
—James 2:15-17

For those who do not love a brother or sister whom they
have seen, cannot love God whom they have not seen. The
commandment we have from him is this: those who love
God must love their brothers and sisters also.
—1 John 4:20-21

Then the righteous will answer him, "Lord, when was it
that we saw you hungry and gave you food, or thirsty and
gave you something to drink? And when was it that we
saw you a stranger and welcomed you, or naked and gave
you clothing? And when was it that we saw you sick or in
prison and visited you?" And the king will answer them,
"Truly I tell you, just as you did it to one of the least of
these who are members of my family, you did it to me."
—Matthew 25:37-40

Responding to God's Call

I am the vine, you are the branches.
—John 15:5

Jesus asked them, "How many loaves have you?" They said, "Seven, and a few small fish."
—Matthew 15:34

Then I heard the voice of the Lord saying, "Whom shall I send, and who will go for us?" And I said, "Here am I; send me!"
—Isaiah 6:8

Prepare the way of the Lord,
make his paths straight.
—Luke 3:4

A Samaritan woman came to draw water, and Jesus said to her, "Give me a drink."
—John 4:7

I came to bring fire to the earth, and how I wish it were already kindled!
—Luke 12:49

Keep Going!

Not that I have already obtained this or have already reached the goal; but I press on to make it my own, because Christ Jesus has made me his own. Beloved, I do not consider that I have made it my own; but this one thing I do: forgetting what lies behind and straining forward to what lies ahead, I press on toward the goal for the prize of the heavenly call of God in Christ Jesus.
—Philippians 3:12-14

By your endurance you will gain your souls.
—Luke 21:19

Be patient, therefore, beloved, until the coming of the
Lord. The farmer waits for the precious crop from the
earth, being patient with it until it receives the early and
the late rains. You also must be patient. Strengthen your
hearts, for the coming of the Lord is near.
—James 5:7-8

I keep the LORD always before me;
because he is at my right hand, I shall not be moved.
—Psalm 16:8

Those who wait for the LORD shall renew their strength,
they shall mount up with wings like eagles,
they shall run and not be weary,
they shall walk and not faint.
—Isaiah 40:31

My brothers and sisters, whenever you face trials of any
kind, consider it nothing but joy, because you know that
the testing of your faith produces endurance; and let
endurance have its full effect, so that you may be mature
and complete, lacking in nothing.
—James 1:2-4

About the Authors

Merle Ankrum lives in North Dakota. His favorite Scripture verse is Jesus' promise: "My sheep hear my voice. I know them, and they follow me. I give them eternal life, and they will never perish. No one will snatch them out of my hand" (John 10:27-28).

Nancy Baker resides in College Station, Texas, with her husband of forty-five years and two cats. She retired from Texas A&M University, where she was a program coordinator and trainer. Since then, she has pursued her lifelong love of writing and has been published in national magazines and anthologies; she is currently writing her grandmother's biography. Nancy directs her parish's ministry to the sick and is a hospice and prison ministry volunteer. Psalms is her favorite book of Scripture.

Magdalen (Maggie) Barrick is a member of St. Francis of Assisi Parish, Baltimore, Maryland, a Third Order Secular Franciscan, and a catechist. A secretary, she enjoys traveling, walking, reading, and concerts. Favorite book of the Bible: the Gospel of John, "especially the Resurrection story."

James Birong has been a dentist in Carrollton, Ohio, and a member of Our Lady of Mercy Parish for thirty years. He has taught CCD for twenty-five years and is very involved with youth groups. For the past seven years, he has also traveled to Haiti for missionary work. He and his wife Ruth have been married thirty-five years and have three children and fourteen grandchildren. "John 14 speaks the truth of our faith to me every time I read it."

Helen Bloodgood is a member of St. Paul of the Cross Parish, Silver Island, Florida. She and her husband James have two daughters and a granddaughter. An aerobics instructor, seamstress, and artist, she enjoys hiking, scuba diving, and fishing. With her daughter, she has developed and organized the Women on Watch Foundation to educate people about violent assault and to help survivors of assaults (www.womenonwatch.org). A frequent speaker, she has appeared in a twelve-minute NBC-TV special, "A Survivor's Story." Helen especially likes the Book of Sirach.

Jack Butler and his wife "Sam" are members of Sacred Heart Parish in Wichita Falls, Texas. They coordinate the area Pre-Cana program and attend the Light of Christ Institute in the Diocese of Fort Worth. Jack is a retired Air Force colonel and maintains a private practice at Rose Street Mental Health Care.

Esperanza Calderon is a retired elementary school teacher who tutors part time for the Chicago Board of Education. An affiliate of the Servants of the Holy Heart of Mary, she is a parishioner at St. Gall's Parish in Chicago and lectors at weekday Masses. She has seven children, eighteen grandchildren, and two great-grandchildren.

Janice Carleton and her husband Jim spent most of their twenty-eight years of married life as very active members of St. John the Baptist Parish, Chico, California. Janice headed a women's Bible study and a prayer group and led worship at Mass. She has recorded a CD of piano meditation music: "It came to me after a priest blessed me, saying that God had a special gift for me. God has also blessed us with four incredible children who are the joy of our lives." With the children now in their twenties and out on their own, Jim and Janice have moved to Portland, Oregon, and look forward to seeing what the Lord has in store in this new phase of life.

Caroline Cella has been married forty years and has a son and daughter and five grandchildren. She was a religion teacher for eight years and a parish director of adult formation for three years. She now works for the Diocese of Rockville Centre, New York, as coordinator of collaborative formation in the Office of Laity and Family. Caroline has a special love for the Book of Isaiah—"inspiration through hard times and many promises of God's love."

Ria Coppens grew up in a small village in the north of Holland. The second oldest of thirteen children, she left school to help her mother when she was in the seventh grade. In 1957, knowing practically no English, she immigrated to Canada with her husband and children. A mother of five and grandmother of twelve, Ria says her children "have been my teachers in many ways and still challenge me to learn." She is an avid gardener, likes crafts of all kinds, and writes poetry and short stories "just as a way to express myself."

Anne Costa and her husband Mike have been married fourteen years and have a seven-year-old daughter, Mary Grace. Anne administers a program that helps people who are blind or visually impaired to find employment. She also works with children and young adults. "I love to write, treasure my Catholic faith, and am especially devoted to Our Lady." Her current writing project: a booklet entitled *Bead by Bead: Praying the Rosary through Depression.*

Patricia Cutie is a member of St. Peter's Parish, Beaufort, South Carolina, and is especially committed to praying before the Blessed Sacrament at perpetual Eucharistic adoration. Married to her husband Tom for forty-four years, she is the mother of three sons and a daughter and a grandmother of eleven. The Book of Wisdom is among her favorites.

Flora De La Torre and her husband Henry are members of Holy Angels Parish, Globe, Arizona. Married in 1950, they have four sons, two daughters, ten grandchildren, and three great-grandchildren. Among her very favorite Bible passages: the Annunciation to Mary (Luke 1:26-38). "This is the greatest miracle and will fill us with awe and understanding, if we believe." Now seventy-eight, Flora says she is "still spreading the Good News to anyone who will listen."

Joanne Dugan and her husband Jim live in a retirement community in Ocala, Florida, and belong to the Queen of Peace Parish community. They have five adult children. Joanne's belief "that life is precious at all stages" has led her to volunteer in ministries focused on helping children and the disabled, elderly, sick, and unborn. Currently, she is a Eucharistic minister at a nearby nursing facility and to the homebound.

Vicky Galczynski is a registered nurse and currently a stay-at-home mom. She and her husband Paul have two sons, Andrew, eleven, and Garrett, five. She belongs to Saint Mark's Parish in Fallston, Maryland, where she enjoys teaching first-grade religious education classes.

Roy Galvan is Director of Maintenance and Grounds, Beeville Independent School District, Beeville, Texas.

Judy Grivas lives in Aberdeen, New Jersey. She and her husband Phil have been married thirty-six years and have one adult son. A writer, she is also an avid reader, crocheter, and animal lover. Favorite book of the Bible: "Colossians, because of its practical as well as spiritual application." (Another version of Judy's article, "Praying with a King," appeared in the August 2001 issue of *New Covenant* magazine.)

Jean Hampton is a retired teacher, a mother of three, and grandmother of four. She worships at St. John's Catholic Church, Old Saybrook, Connecticut, and reads and studies the Bible every day. She is partial to Psalm 1, 1 Corinthians 13, and the Gospel of John.

Gabriel Harkay was a cadet in the technical officer training school of the Hungarian Army during the last years of World War II and volunteered for active duty at age sixteen. Following the war, he escaped from Hungary and eventually became a professional mechanical engineer registered in California and Louisiana. In 1964, he became a professed member of the Third Order of St. Francis— a commitment which, he says, has inspired his involvement in activities such as CCD, Cursillo, and Marriage Encounter. Gabriel and his wife recently celebrated their fiftieth anniversary together with their four children, seven grandchildren, and a few close friends. "Daily Scripture meditation and Mass, along with weekly prayer meetings, are the framework of my present spiritual life."

Paul Harvey grew up in England in the Midlands, and came to the United States eleven years ago. Married with two young children, he works in information technology for the U.S. government. A musician, Paul plays the guitar, leads worship, and writes praise and worship songs. He has recorded two albums for The Word Among Us: *I Will Sing to Your Name* and *Behold!*, both available at www.wordamongus.org. His favorite book of the Bible is Psalms.

Ann Hegelheimer is a member of Holy Angels Catholic Church, in St. Thomas, Ontario, and has participated in various aspects of parish life—among them the Catholic Women's League, prayer groups, the decorating committee, ushering, a weekly Bible study, and the religious and spiritual care board for a local nursing home. "I also enjoy artwork, painting, and crafts, as well as playing cards and gardening."

Doris Biel Herter is retired and has six children and twelve grandchildren. She attends Holy Trinity Catholic Church in Louisville, Kentucky, and completed a ministry formation program there a few years ago. She is a regular participant in a Sunday program where "the Scriptures for the day are discussed, along with how they apply to our lives." Doris also helps with the children's liturgy and with summer vacation Bible school. Her favorite Bible book is John.

Kathleen Hervochon is a special education teacher and a member of St. Patrick's Parish in Newcastle, Maine. She and her husband, George, have three grown daughters.

Michael Ho is married with three children and serves as a Eucharistic minister and facilitator of the RCIA team at Fatima Church, Kuala Lumpur. Now retired, he keeps fit through TaiChi and Chinese QiGong. He has a special interest in Bible study and is especially drawn to "all four Gospels, the prophetic books of Hosea, Ezekiel, Jeremiah and Isaiah, and Psalms and Proverbs."

Rosemarie Hunt spent years deciphering conflicting medical advice about her son ("Stocking Up," Chapter 8), but it led her to a masters degree and into a twenty-five-year career in special education teaching and administration. Now retired, she and her husband are lectors and teach in the RCIA and the parish education program at St. Mary/St. James Church in Charlestown, Rhode Island. Rosemarie spends two days a week with Literacy Volunteers of America and one day a week at the parish food pantry. The Hunts have two "homemade" sons and one daughter whom they adopted from Vietnam in 1972. "We have one grandson and are hoping for more!"

Michael Iwuchukwu belongs to St. Albert the Great Parish, in Obosi, Nigeria, and "by the grace of God" is a regional coordinator in the Singles for Christ renewal movement. A pharmaceuticals salesman, he comes from a family of ten children—"all of us practicing Catholics"—and enjoys Christian books and gospel music. John 3:16 is his favorite Scripture verse.

Bruce Johnson is active at Catholic Information Center's Chapel of St. Paul in Grand Rapids, Michigan. He serves on its education committee and participates in its efforts to relocate Somali Bantu refugee families. He is a lawyer working for the Michigan courts and, at fifty-one, "tries to keep up" with his sons—eleven-year-old Christian and seventeen-year-old Mark—on the baseball diamond. Favorite Bible verse: Romans 8:28.

Juliana Jones has a degree in agriculture from West Virginia University and at one time specialized in plant propagation. "Eventually I switched to propagation of children, and yet again to propagation of the faith." Juli continues to mature in faith through theological studies in Education for Parish Service

(EPS), a program providing academic and spiritual growth for lay Catholics. "I am a big fan of Salesian spirituality and its aspect of spiritual friendship."

Rita M. Keylor is a retired dental hygienist who comes from a family of nine children—"all of us staunch Catholics." She belongs to Sacred Heart Church, Auburn, Maine, and is a member of its Golden Age Club.

Mary E. Killmond lives in Woodland Hills, California, teaches religion and Scripture in a Catholic high school, and is "very involved in my parish."

Joseph Komban studied mechanical engineering in Kerala, India, and has done post-graduate work in marine engineering and management. With twenty-eight years' experience in the field, he now heads a marine service business. He and his wife, Victoria Joseph, have one daughter, Christina Joseph. Active in his parish and in a Franciscan association, Joseph has a special interest in writing and has some book projects in mind. He loves the Gospels and says that "personal meditation in the night is a habit."

Tom Krulikowski is an engineering manager and a "happily married father of two teenage daughters." A parishioner of St. Louise de Marillac Church, in Pittsburgh, Pennsylvania, he is a cantor and a member of the contemporary and traditional choirs. "I also enjoy bicycling with friends. We typically cycle fifty to seventy-five miles a week and do occasional one-hundred-and fifty-mile bike tours in a weekend."

Isagani L. Landicho retired from government service ten years ago. He keeps himself occupied and tranquil by working in his small garden, where, as a "hydroponics enthusiast," he grows plants in nutrient solutions. "What brings me the most peace and gratification is serving as a lay minister of the Lord in my parish of Santa Maria della Strada, in Quezon City, the Philippines." Isagani and his wife also belong to a Catholic charismatic community. John 15:1-10, his favorite Scripture passage, inspires him to maintain grapevines, "a novelty that does not normally grow in my country. My grapevines remind me of God's love and encourage me to be one with him."

Jeanne Legault lives in Ponteix, Saskatchewan, Canada. Married forty-seven years, she has five children and twelve grandchildren. She has been involved in community projects, served on the parish council, and participated in various types of church ministry, including many years with youth groups. She has a collection of angel figures that now includes four hundred items.

Jane T. Leischer ("My Two Joshuas," Chapter 9) has been cancer free for five years. "I praise God for every sunrise, enjoy gardening, and delight in our six grandchildren. God is with us."

Lisa Levy and her husband, who is a deacon in the Catholic Church, have five children and live in Port Byron, Illinois. Lisa's interests include reading, Bible study, and listening to music. She is active in Cursillo and pro-life work. Scripture favorites are Psalms and Proverbs.

Cecilia Martin is a member of St. Joseph's Church in Winchester, Indiana, and serves on the parish finance council. For many years, she was a parish religious education teacher and director and, with her husband, coordinated CYO activities. A registered nurse with a masters degree in health services administration, she works at Henry County Memorial Hospital in New Castle, Indiana. Cecilia grew up in a family of ten children and is especially grateful to have had "very devout Catholic parents who showed us how to bring God into our lives on a daily basis." She and her husband have been married thirty-three years; they have two children and three grandchildren.

Sr. Virgene Marx, O.S.B., a Benedictine sister living in an Ogden, Utah, monastery, was the youngest of fourteen children raised by "strong German, staunch Catholic" parents. "Two boys became priests and two girls entered religious life—all Benedictines. The others married, and I have wonderful nieces and nephews." Sr. Virgene spent her life in hospital work—as a registered nurse, certified nurse anesthetist, and certified chaplain. A certified spiritual director, she oversees the monastery's Oblate program and also volunteers in the alcohol and drug rehabilitation program at Ogden Regional Medical Center. "I celebrated my Golden Jubilee five years ago. As I look back on my life with its joys, difficulties, and mistakes, I know that God was with me all the time, though I did not always realize it. I have come to realize that God guides me every moment of the day—if I let him. I am a very happy and grateful Benedictine sister."

Norma J. Matasich and her husband, Robert, have three teenage children. An office manager, she attends St. Jude's in Hampstead, North Carolina, and teaches faith formation to fifth graders. Norma enjoys reading and says her favorite Bible books are Proverbs and John's Gospel.

John Mitchell is married with four children and has been teaching math and computer science for over twenty-five years in a Fairfax County, Virginia, public high school. He is a member of St. Philip's Parish in Falls Church, where he has been a lector and has been involved in youth ministry. His favorite book of the Bible is the Gospel of John, and his favorite verse in that Gospel is John 17:21, "that they may all be one," because it holds out hope for Christian unity.

Lorrenne Mulherin is a widow with three grown sons and nine grandchildren. After living on a farm all her life, she recently moved to the city of Cedar Rapids, Iowa, where she is very actively involved at St. Jude's Church. She gives talks, helps with funerals, mentors, leads a Bible study, serves on the spiritual growth committee, and is in the third year of a lay formation program. "My life is far from boring! I have been blessed to experience God throughout my life. I enjoy sharing the blessings with others and am writing them down for my grandchildren and great-grandchildren."

Katherine Murphy, the mother of two grown sons, is a fifteen-year breast cancer survivor and freelance writer. She lives with her husband in Clifton Park, New York, and is a member of St. Edward the Confessor Church. Portions of her story, "Asleep No More" have been excerpted from her book, *Awake, O Sleeper: How I Rediscovered God through Breast Cancer* (Sun Creek Books, 2003. Available at www.amazon.com and www.bn.com).

Fr. Carlo Notaro, D.S. Carn., has been a priest in the Order of St. Camillus, the Servants of the Sick, for approximately fifteen years. He holds a doctorate in pastoral theology related to health care and works with the elderly at St. Camillus Campus, Wauwatosa, Wisconsin, and as a volunteer chaplain at Children's Hospital in Milwaukee. He also teaches a course in spirituality, writes articles for Catholic magazines, gives talks, and "most importantly," helps his elderly mother.

Uche Mercy Okonkwo, Ph.D. received her doctorate from Teachers College, Columbia University, New York, and works at a university in Lagos, Nigeria. Teacher education, language education, and curriculum and instruction are her areas of specialization. Special interests are Scripture reading and advocacy on behalf of the needy. She has a fourteen-year-old daughter, Ifeoma Mary Marvella.

Ludy Z. Pardo is an economics officer at the Asian Development Bank based in Manila, the Philippines. She and her husband, Lito, have one grown daughter, Rashel Yasmin, an urban planner. They are active members of a Catholic renewal community—the Brotherhood of Christian Businessmen and Professionals— which aims to evangelize people who work in business or in the professions. Ludy enjoys gardening and reading spiritual books and finds special inspiration in Jeremiah 29:11-15.

Barbara A. Ramian was a parish director of religious education for eighteen years. In her current position as associate director of religious education for the Diocese of Worcester, Massachusetts, she has special responsibility for parish high school and Confirmation programs and for catechetical leadership. "I love Scripture, especially the Hebrew Scriptures, and enjoy reflecting on the ways in which these books, written so long ago, are so relevant to the joys and struggles we face in our lives today."

Evelyn Richter is a member of St. Stanislaus Church, in Bandera, Texas, and heads the parish's "get well" committee. Her favorite Scripture books: Psalms and the Gospels.

Rev. Harriet E. Rodriguez holds masters degrees in public administration and urban ministry and was ordained at God's

House of Prayer in Raleigh, North Carolina, in 1999. She does social work at the Visiting Nurse Service in New York City and is associate minister of Christian education at New York's Mount Pleasant Community Church. Her son teaches at City College and is completing a Ph.D. program. For recreation, "I love to bowl and like going to football, baseball, tennis, and basketball games."

Herbert Rodriguez lives in Miami, Florida, and is vice president of a distributor for a major corporation. As an accomplished commercial pilot with multiple ratings, he enjoys many outdoor activities—"being on the golf course and in the ocean are my favorites." Herb, his wife Ofelia, and their five-year-old, Michelle, are parishioners at Sts. Peter and Paul Catholic Church in Miami.

Kathy Ann Rogers is a member of St. Victor's Catholic Church in Gibraltar, Michigan. She has been an American Cancer Society "Reach for Recovery" counselor since June 2003.

Aline Rousseau-Zunti is a retired teacher and mother of eleven children. She lives in Alberta, Canada, and is active in her parish as a Mass server and a member of the Catholic Women's League. During the nine years when she was a widow, she served on a "New Beginnings" team that gave weekend retreats for people who were widowed, separated, or divorced. "I remarried nineteen and a half years ago. We have thirty-four grandchildren and are expecting our twenty-first great-grandchild in January 2004."

Mark Sandore is serving a sentence at Groveland Correctional Facility, Sonyea, New York. A music lover, he sings in the prison choir and is teaching himself classical guitar. He enjoys drawing and watercolors, golf and the outdoors, gardening and spiritual reading ("Thomas Merton is a favorite"). "Once I am released, I plan on getting involved in a prison ministry for ex-felons returning to society." Marks hopes "that the Holy Spirit will use my story to bless someone the way he has so often blessed me during my incarceration."

Donna Serna-Lopez is a nurse and has a daughter and granddaughter. A member of St. Ignatius Loyola Catholic Community, in Denver, Colorado, she lectors, teaches religious education, serves on the liturgy committee, and hopes to work with the parish RCIA program. She is a graduate of the Catholic Biblical School in Denver and says that "studying Scripture has been the most important thing I've done for myself."

Kathleen Shanahan resides in Westerly, Rhode Island, with her children, eighteen-year-old Brendan and sixteen-year-old Briana. A daily communicant at Immaculate Conception Church, she is a lector and Eucharistic minister who also does volunteer work such as visiting shut-ins and facilitating a bereavement support group. "Our parish is blessed to have a perpetual adoration chapel, and I feel fortunate for the time I spend there with Jesus."

Janice L. Smith works at Tufts University. She and her husband have been married for thirty-seven years and have three grown children and five grandchildren. Both are actively involved parishioners of Sacred Heart Catholic Church in Medford Hillside, Massachusetts, and serve in various volunteer capacities. A certified pastoral minister, Janice is a Benedictine Oblate of Glastonbury Abbey, Hingham, Massachusetts. "You have turned my mourning into dancing" (Psalm 30:11) is a Scripture verse with special resonance: "The most profound joy and blessing of my life has been to search for and find my firstborn daughter, whom I had surrendered for adoption thirty-one years prior. My heart was indeed filled to overflowing, to see her face again."

Dianne Spotts retired early, in May 2000, attended creative writing classes, joined a writers' group, and saw her first paid article published in the October 2000 issue of *Senior Connection*, a Catholic quarterly. A parish musician for twenty-eight years, she also writes for her parish quarterly newsletter and serves on a committee to welcome Catholics who are returning to the faith. Her great desire is that "all my fellow Catholics get into the word of God so that God's Word will find a happy home in them and light their path." Dianne is married and has four children and ten grandchildren.

Dave Steeples has served on twelve Cursillo weekends—including one given at the Federal Correctional Center in Pekin, Illinois, whose theme was his favorite verse: "You did not choose me, but I chose you" (John 15:16). With his wife Lorie, he recently began a four-year spiritual formation program. For Dave, it will culminate in his ordination as a deacon in the diocese of Peoria, Illinois.

Heather Stevinson and her husband Michael have two young children—twenty-two-month-old Joseph and two-month-old Anna—and live in the Springfield, Illinois, area. Heather is a busy "stay-at-home wife and mother."

Lillian Valencia and her husband are very active members of St. Mary's Church in Farmington, New Mexico, and also are part of a jail ministry. "What we receive is more than what we give."

Lillian is a quilter, and her husband is active in Senior Olympics—
"number one in 8-Ball this year!"

Jennifer Waroway is a fifth-grade teacher at St. John Brebeuf
Catholic School in Winnipeg, Manitoba, Canada. Jennifer enjoys
seeing the world through the eyes of children.

Davin Winger and his wife Teague belong to Sacred Heart of
Jesus Parish in Spearman, Texas, where they currently serve as
directors of religious education. Married twenty years, they
have three children—Ryan, Reid, and Leigh Anne. Davin also
works with high school youth and adult faith enrichment.
Biblical favorite is the Gospel of John, especially chapter 17. "And
Philippians 2:5-11 is an awesome passage—I can't help but be
amazed when I read it." Davin writes a weekly e-mail newsletter of personal thoughts and musings and will gladly send it to
anyone who requests it (dwinger@gruver.net).